The
Dust Bowl

The Dust Bowl

Therese DeAngelis
and Gina DeAngelis

CHELSEA HOUSE PUBLISHERS
Philadelphia

Frontispiece: Huge duststorms, called "rollers," plagued the Midwest United States during the 1930s, and devestated a once thriving agricultural economy.

CHELSEA HOUSE PUBLISHERS

Editor in Chief Sally Cheney
Director of Production Kim Shinners
Production Manager Pamela Loos
Art Director Sara Davis
Production Editor Diann Grasse

Staff for THE DUST BOWL

Editor Bill Conn
Picture Researcher Pat Holl
Layout by 21st Century Publishing and Communications, Inc.

First Printing

1 3 5 7 9 8 6 4 2

The Chelsea House World Wide Web address is
http://www.chelseahouse.com

Library of Congress Cataloging-in-Publication Data

DeAngelis, Therese.
    The Dust Bowl / Therese DeAngelis and Gina DeAngelis.
       p. cm — (Great disasters, reforms and ramifications)
    Includes bibliographical references and index.
    Contents: The end of the world — The breadbasket of the world — Trouble in wheat heaven – Mean skies and hard times — The Okie migration — A New Deal for the Dust Bowl — The rains return.
       ISBN: 0-7910-6323-2 (alk. paper)
       1. Dust storms—Great Plains—History—20th century—Juvenile literature. 2. Droughts—Great Plains—History—20th century—Juvenile literature. 3. Great Plains—Social conditions—20th century—Juvenile literature. 4. Depressions—1929—Great Plains—Juvenile literature. 5. Farmers—Great Plains—Social conditions—20th century—Juvenile literature. 6. Agriculture—Social aspects—Great Plains—History—20th century—Juvenile literature. [1. Dust storms—Great Plains. 2. Droughts—Great Plains—History. 3. Depressions—1929. 4. Agriculture—Great Plains—History. 5. Great Plains—History.] I. DeAngelis, Gina. II. Title. III. Series.

F595 .D35 2001
978' .03—dc21
                                          2001047596

Contents

GREAT DISASTERS
REFORMS and RAMIFICATIONS

Jill McCaffrey
National Chairman
Armed Forces Emergency Services
American Red Cross

Introduction

Disasters have always been a source of fascination and awe. Tales of a great flood that nearly wipes out all life are among humanity's oldest recorded stories, dating at least from the second millennium B.C., and they appear in cultures from the Middle East to the Arctic Circle to the southernmost tip of South America and the islands of Polynesia. Typically gods are at the center of these ancient disaster tales—which is perhaps not too surprising, given the fact that the tales originated during a time when human beings were at the mercy of natural forces they did not understand.

To a great extent, we still are at the mercy of nature, as anyone who reads the newspapers or watches nightly news broadcasts can attest.

Hurricanes, earthquakes, tornados, wildfires, and floods continue to exact a heavy toll in suffering and death, despite our considerable knowledge of the workings of the physical world. If science has offered only limited protection from the consequences of natural disasters, it has in no way diminished our fascination with them. Perhaps that's because the scale and power of natural disasters force us as individuals to confront our relatively insignificant place in the physical world and remind us of the fragility and transience of our lives. Perhaps it's because we can imagine ourselves in the midst of dire circumstances and wonder how we would respond. Perhaps it's because disasters seem to bring out the best and worst instincts of humanity: altruism and selfishness, courage and cowardice, generosity and greed.

As one of the national chairmen of the American Red Cross, a humanitarian organization that provides relief for victims of disasters, I have had the privilege of seeing some of humanity's best instincts. I have witnessed communities pulling together in the face of trauma; I have seen thousands of people answer the call to help total strangers in their time of need.

Of course, helping victims after a tragedy is not the only way, or even the best way, to deal with disaster. In many cases planning and preparation can minimize damage and loss of life—or even avoid a disaster entirely. For, as history repeatedly shows, many disasters are caused not by nature but by human folly, shortsightedness, and unethical conduct. For example, when a land developer wanted to create a lake for his exclusive resort club in Pennsylvania's Allegheny Mountains in 1880, he ignored expert warnings and cut corners in reconstructing an earthen dam. On May 31, 1889, the dam gave way, unleashing 20 million tons of water on the towns below. The Johnstown Flood, the deadliest in American history, claimed more than 2,200 lives. Greed and negligence would figure prominently in the Triangle Shirtwaist Company fire in 1911. Deplorable conditions in the garment sweatshop, along with a failure to give any thought to the safety of workers, led to the tragic deaths of 146 persons. Technology outstripped wisdom only a year later, when the designers of the luxury liner *Titanic* smugly declared their state-of-the-art ship "unsinkable," seeing no need to provide lifeboat capacity for everyone onboard. On the night of April 14, 1912, more than 1,500 passengers and crew paid for this hubris with their lives after the ship collided with an iceberg and sank. But human catastrophes aren't always the unforeseen consequences of carelessness or folly. In the 1940s the leaders of Nazi Germany purposefully and systematically set out to exterminate all Jews, along with Gypsies, homosexuals, the mentally ill, and other so-called undesirables. More recently terrorists have targeted random members of society, blowing up airplanes and buildings in an effort to advance their political agendas.

The books in the GREAT DISASTERS: REFORMS AND RAMIFICATIONS series examine these and other famous disasters, natural and human made. They explain the causes of the disasters, describe in detail how events unfolded, and paint vivid portraits of the people caught up in dangerous circumstances. But these books are more than just accounts of what happened to whom and why. For they place the disasters in historical perspective, showing how people's attitudes and actions changed and detailing the steps society took in the wake of each calamity. And in the end, the most important lesson we can learn from any disaster—as well as the most fitting tribute to those who suffered and died—is how to avoid a repeat in the future.

The End of the World

The area called the "breadbasket of the world"—Texas, Kansas, Oklahoma, New Mexico, and Colorado—was so drought-stricken in the 1930s that it became known as the "Dust Bowl." Here, a giant storm of flying topsoil threatens to engulf a small farm in Oklahoma.

"The Lord shall make the rain of thy land powder and dust, from heaven it shall come down upon thee, until thou be destroyed."

—Bible verse often quoted by Dust Bowl victims

April 14, 1935 dawned clear and sunny, with a gentle breeze. Farmers and their families in the large area around which Kansas, Oklahoma, Texas, New Mexico, and Colorado converge were glad to see the sun. For several years, since the dry season of 1931, frequent windstorms had made the air thick and the sky black with dust. The region was in the midst of a severe drought, and this spring the dust storms had been particularly bad.

Farmers and townspeople in the region had become accustomed to the terrible "dirt blizzards." They simply tied pieces of cloth over their noses and mouths and went on with their work, if they could. They had known people who had gotten lost in their own yards when big storms blew up; some had even died. They knew neighbors who got sick from breathing in all the dirt; some of them also died, of a strange respiratory illness they called "dust pneumonia." The atmosphere was almost always heavy with fine-grained particles of soil, thanks to the ever-present prairie winds that blew the loose topsoil into the air. People learned not to stray too far from home because at any moment a storm might blow, and in the darkness they might never find their way back.

Today, on Palm Sunday, it was different for a change—the air was clear and the sun blazed. People could finally go to church, visit friends and neighbors, and do outdoor chores that they'd been unable to finish because of the dust storms. Near the town of Hooker, Oklahoma, several hundred people joined forces on a "rabbit drive." Since the drought began in 1931, the wild jackrabbit population had soared. Nobody quite knew why, since there wasn't enough food for people, let alone all those rabbits. They had reproduced so rapidly, however, that they were now a constant menace, eating the few grasses and crops the farmers could coax into growing in the dry, loose soil. In some places, the jackrabbits took over the land entirely: "Just looked like the country below us just . . . all began to move," one man recalls as he came over a hill. "Looked like a herd of sheep, but it was jackrabbits." As a last resort, the residents of the area took drastic measures to decrease their numbers.

During rabbit drives, a large group of people would

The jackrabbit population soared in the Dust Bowl, eating the little vegetation that the farmers could coax from the arid ground. Residents were forced to kill the jackrabbits to ensure their own survival, and used the meat to feed their starving families.

surround hundreds of jackrabbits and corral them into a small area. When the trapped rabbits tried to run out of the human circle, they were clubbed to death. (Guns were forbidden on the drives because they were unsafe with so many people participating.) Many people felt that they had no choice: making a living off the parched land in the midst of a long drought was difficult enough without jackrabbits destroying the few remaining crops. It was a question of survival: the rabbits or them. Besides, the jackrabbits provided much-needed meat for poor families.

At 4 P.M. on April 14, the rabbit drivers of Hooker were about to close their circle when someone looked to the horizon. A huge, boiling, black cloud of dust was bearing down on the crowd. There was no place to run, no shelter nearby, and the towering "roller" (the nickname given to dust storms) was headed their way. Everyone sat down, covered their faces as best they could, and prayed. The rabbits and the horses the participants had been riding stumbled about, crying in the murk. It was as though the very air had turned to sand, and the wind whipped the stinging crystals of dirt into faces, eyes, ears, mouths, under clothing and shoes—everywhere.

Hooker residents who were closer to home saw the gigantic cloud coming and ran for cover. Lawrence Svobida, a Kansas farmer, later published a book called *An Empire of Dust*, describing his experiences in the 1930s. He created a vivid portrait of what a roller looked like as it appeared on the horizon:

> Already it has the banked appearance of a cumulus cloud, but it is black instead of white, and it hangs low, seeming to hug the earth. Instead of being slow to change its form, it appears to be rolling on itself from the crest downward. As it sweeps onward, the landscape is progressively blotted out. Birds fly in terror before the storm, and only those that are strong of wind may escape. The smaller birds fly until they are exhausted, then fall to the ground, to share the fate of the thousands of jackrabbits which perish from suffocation.

Farm families had grown accustomed to the storms by 1935. They were used to sleeping with cloths covering their noses and mouths, used to putting petroleum jelly in their nostrils, used to wetting towels and cloths and bunching them up around window frames and under doors. None of it helped much. They'd even seen big storms before—in November 1933 and May 1934. The past March had been particularly dusty too. But this storm was something else. It was enormous—bigger than any they'd ever seen. People hunkered down in their houses, stores, wherever they could, and listened helplessly to the howling wind and blowing dust.

Melt White, a farmer's son, remembered seeing the great roller on the distant horizon that day. "[I]n the north it was just a little bank, oh, like about eight or ten feet high," he recalls. "It had one of those headers out on each end, you know. . . . [A]nd I said, 'Dad, we ain't goin' to be able to go to church tonight.'" During the storm, Melt remembers, even though he was safely indoors, "the wind kept blowing harder and harder. It kept getting darker and darker. And the old house is just a-vibratin' like it was gonna blow away. And I started trying to see my hand. And I kept bringing my hand up closer and closer and closer and closer. And I finally touched the end of my nose and I still couldn't see my hand. That's how black it was. A lot of people got out of bed, got their children out of the bed. Got down praying, thought that was it. They thought that was the end of the world."

Many others who saw the immense roller and heard the thundering wind that day later said that they too believed the world was ending. It wasn't just Texas, Kansas, and Oklahoma that suffered, however. In a diary entry 11 days later, Ann Marie Low, a farmer's daughter in North

Dakota, recorded her memories of the April 14 storm:

> Last weekend was the worst dust storm we ever had. We've been having quite a bit of blowing dirt every year since the drouth [drought] started, not only here, but all over the Great Plains. Many days this spring the air is just full of dirt coming, literally, for hundreds of miles. It sifts into everything. After we wash the dishes and put them away, so much dust sifts into the cupboards we must wash them again before the next meal. Clothes in the closets are covered with dust.
>
> Last weekend no one was taking an automobile out for fear of ruining the motor. I rode Roany to Frank's place to return a gear. To find my way I had to ride right beside the fence scarcely able to see from one fence post to the next.

The storm on April 14, 1935 was so vast and extended so high into the atmosphere over the Midwestern United States that it blackened the skies over eastern cities, including New York, Philadelphia, and Washington, D.C., and dropped silt on ships in the Atlantic Ocean. The rest of the United States had only recently become aware of the misery that Great Plains residents had been suffering for years. Just two weeks before Black Sunday, *TIME* magazine reported on the stark contrast between the daily lives of East Coast residents and those of Plains farmers:

> As March sunlight gilded their breakfast tables, Washingtonians read in their morning papers that in about two weeks the Japanese cherry trees around the Tidal Basin would be in full bloom. The same day Kansans breakfasted by lamp light and read in their morning papers that one of the worst dust storms in the history

"Rollers," or dust storms, posed great threats to residents living in the Dust Bowl. Many people suffocated when caught far from home with no place to take shelter against these storms.

of their State was weeping darkly overhead. Damp sheets hung over the windows, but table cloths were grimy. . . . Food had a gritty taste. Dirt drifted around doorways like snow. People who ventured outside coughed and choked as the fields of Kansas, Colorado,

The dust storm that hung over the Midwest on April 14, 1935 was so large and extended so high into the atmosphere that it darkened the skies as far east as New York City.

Wyoming, Nebraska and Oklahoma rose and took flight through the windy air.

During last week's dust storm, which . . . in the heart of the drought district ran on for twelve consecutive days, police closed highways to prevent accidents. Airplanes were grounded. Schools and businesses were closed. Health officers advised every one to stay at home. Three children and several adults were reported dead of pneumonia after breathing dust. . . . [R]ailway traffic was at a standstill. When high winds swept the dust Eastward Kansas City had night at midday and people walked the streets with handkerchiefs tied across their faces. How great was the crop damage remained largely a matter of guesswork. Oklahoma grimly reported that 50% of the wheat in the Western part of the State was ruined.

With each violent dust storm, the topsoil of drought-stricken Texas, Kansas, Oklahoma, and neighboring states was carried away on the wind. Because of these storms, an area so fertile that it had been dubbed "the breadbasket of the world" became known instead, during the 1930s, as the "Dust Bowl."

The Breadbasket of the World

The Great Plains, the area
in the United States where
the Dust Bowl occurred,
encompass a variety of
landscapes including
canyons, plateaus, forests,
mesas, and mountains. Its
most dominant feature is
the grassland, seen in the
foreground of this picture.
Grasslands once stretched
over a million square miles
of the Great Plains

W hat could have caused the devastation of the Dust Bowl in the Midwest? How did such a widespread drought occur? How could so many dust storms have rolled through Oklahoma, Kansas, Texas, and other states during the 1930s? We can find part of the answers by examining the kind of land where the drought and dust storms occurred: the high plains region of the Great Plains.

The Great Plains stretch from Mexico to Canada, and from the Rocky Mountains to the Mississippi River Valley. They encompass parts of 13 U.S. states (Colorado, Iowa, Kansas, Minnesota, Missouri, Montana, Nebraska, New Mexico, North and South Dakota, Oklahoma, Texas, and Wyoming) and at least three Canadian provinces (Alberta, Saskatchewan, and Manitoba). Far from being the bland and featureless expanse most people imagine, the Great Plains are made up of a variety of landscapes, including canyons, plateaus, jagged outcrops of rock, forests, mesas, and isolated mountains. The greatest portion of the Plains, however, is made up of several types of grassland. These grasslands were once the largest on earth, covering more than a million square miles. Trees grow only along streams and rivers and in the few mountains in the Black Hills region (the northern Plains). Just south of the grassland and mixed with the grasses are creosote bushes along the Pecos River, and mesquite, oak, and juniper trees farther east.

The Great Plains slope gently eastward, from 6,000 feet above sea level at the foot of the Rocky Mountains to 1,500 feet in the lowlands. Beginning about 570 million years ago, according to geologists, more than 350,000 miles of North America's interior was covered by a shallow sea. It was formed in an "outwash plain" created when rivers and streams carried eroded gravel, sand, and clay from the Rocky Mountains. The sea was prevented from draining by glaciers to the north, but about 70 million years ago, the continent began rising. A series of layered sediments, each 5,000 to 10,000 feet thick, were deposited on the floor of the ocean as the Rocky Mountains continued to erode. Over centuries, the layers of sediment formed rock strata, which now lie nearly horizontal under the Great Plains.

During the Great Ice Age, or Pleistocene era, which ended about 10,000 years ago, ice sheets slowly advanced southward from Canada into the plains of North America. Across river valleys, glaciers shaped the land into a characteristic form: the surface of the valley's far side was "planed" or smoothed, so that it sloped gently, while the near side was carved into steep formations. The glaciers also created moraines—accumulations of earth and stone picked up and carried by the glacier's movement. The ice sheets stopped short of what is now the Great Plains region, in an area called the Central Lowland (mostly between the Ohio and Missouri Rivers). Today, some of the Great Plains borders are marked by escarpments—long, steep cliffs generated by glacier movement. The resulting landscape south of the Central Lowland became a nearly flat region 3,000 to 4,000 feet above sea level—a plateau known today as the high plains.

Anyone familiar with the Great Plains may have difficulty believing that they were once mostly forested. Millions of years ago, bands of spruce and fir grew south of the glaciers. Nebraska and Kansas were part of a "taiga," a subarctic forest that often borders a tundra; groves of white spruce alternated with quaking aspen and meadowlands. Farther south, in present-day northern Texas, spruce, quaking aspen, western hackberry, and other deciduous trees flourished.

Eons before the 1930s, the Great Plains region endured several droughts. During a long arid period in the Pleistocene era, high-velocity winds—fiercer and more protracted than those familiar to modern-day residents—began scouring the area. Sand and fine particles of silt and clay, called "loess," were carried east and south in huge clouds and settled in thick blankets on the upland plains. The deepest loess accumulation was along the Missouri River in western Iowa and northwestern Missouri. In Nebraska, 42,000 square miles of loess were deposited in layers as thick as 20 feet. The rich farmland of Iowa, Illinois, Wisconsin, and Indiana is the result of these huge storms. Heavier, coarser sands were deposited by the winds in dune fields along rivers in the western Plains, including Nebraska and South Dakota.

When did the Great Plains, especially the southern Plains, become primarily grasslands? The transition began between five and seven million years ago, after the great storms. The loess combined with the earth already in place to form two distinct types of soil. One was a dark surface layer of rich organic matter, whose color ranges from dark brown in the western Plains to almost black in the east. The second layer is an alkaline substance called calcium carbonate, a mineral salt formed by the sun's leaching in areas that receive little rain. Where more rain falls, these salts are frequently washed down to groundwater level. In dry regions like the Great Plains, however, this material solidifies and forms a type of crust, or hardpan, beneath the organic soil. This prevents rainwater from reaching the earth below it and keeps deep-rooted plants from taking hold. When moist, this type of soil is rich in minerals; during dry spells it is very easily leached of nutrients.

As glaciers slowly retreated from the Plains, the climate shifted as well. Today, the high plains where the Dust Bowl occurred have a semi-arid climate, which means that the region averages less than 20 inches of precipitation annually. The eastern Plains receive more rainfall than those in the west, in part because of the Arkansas, Canadian, Cimarron, Missouri, Platte, Republican, and Saskatchewan Rivers, which flow eastward in wide, low beds. Most of the rainfall on the Great Plains comes during the growing seasons of spring and summer, but because these are also the seasons in which the temperatures are highest, the rain often evaporates quickly.

On the southern Plains, temperature ranges and precipitation levels are often wildly unpredictable. Floods, cyclones, and blizzards are relatively common, and droughts occur frequently in cycles lasting several years or even decades. The reasons, say meteorologists, have to do with the high-level winds of three powerful weather systems: a mild, dry air mass that crosses the Rocky

Mountains; a cold, dry air mass from the Arctic; and the warm, wet air from the Gulf of Mexico. When and where these systems clash determines the type and severity of the weather on the southern Plains.

Archaeological evidence suggests that humans began migrating from Northeast Asia between 20,000 and 12,000 years ago. These natives, called Paleo-Indians, were nomadic—they followed the migratory patterns of waterfowl and movements of game herds such as caribou, mastodons (prehistoric elephant-like animals), and bison, on which they relied for food. They took shelter in caves, used fire, and fashioned tools out of stone. Roughly 8,000 years ago, the glaciers retreated for the last time and the larger animals became extinct. As the hunters moved eastward and found more stable populations of smaller animals, they also began living in relatively permanent homes. Between 5000 and 1000 B.C., during what historians call the Archaic period, they began settling in river valleys, planting crops, raising domesticated animals, and building their own shelters. Around this time, the inhabitants of North America also began diverging into distinct tribes with separate cultures.

The primary source of food for the various Plains tribes, including the Blackfeet, Cheyenne, Crow, Comanche, Pawnee, and Sioux, came from the abundant herds of bison that roamed the Great Plains. Weighing up to 2,000 pounds and standing more than 12 feet long and up to six feet high at their massive shoulder humps, bison were so vital to Plains Indians that they became a central part of tribal life, revered as a powerful life force. But the Native Americans also used nearly every other part of the animal: they fashioned footwear, clothing, and shelter from the hides, sewed with bison sinew, and carved tools from the animal bones.

Historians estimate that as many as 200 million bison

Two Native Americans cure a bison hide. The bison was an important resource for Native Americans living on the Plains, and every part of the animal was used: meat was eaten, hides were scraped and used as clothing and shelter, and bones were fashioned into tools.

once thundered through the Plains. Bison have great endurance and can run up to 35 miles an hour, so Native Americans devised a number of techniques for capturing them. One method, called a "surround," was to form a circular human chain around a small number of the animals, herding them together so that the hunters had a better shot. Another was the "jump," in which groups of hunters stampeded bison over a cliff. The hunters might also drive the animals into natural traps, such as blind canyons, where they could more easily kill them.

Most important, Native Americans killed only as many bison as they needed to subsist. "The Indian was frugal in the midst of plenty," explains Luther Standing Bear, a member of the Lakota tribe. "When the buffalo roamed the plains in multitudes, he slaughtered only what he could eat and these he used [down] to the hair and bones." Because the Plains Indians killed buffalo sparingly, the bison population remained relatively constant.

Grasslands provided the perfect environment for hoofed herbivores such as bison. (Naturalist Ernest Thompson Seton estimated in 1909 that each bison on the Plains required 30 acres of vegetation to survive.) The enormous expanses of prairie included a wide variety of grasses and grains—the only kinds of vegetation that could survive the region's harsh climate and soil constitution. One historian estimates that out of the roughly 4,500 species of grass that have evolved, the Great Plains were home to several hundred, and up to 75 species took root in one region alone. In the eastern part of the Great Plains, which received the most rain, tall grasses such as big bluestem, switch grass, and Indian grass grew as high as eight feet, with roots nearly six feet deep. In the southern Plains, however, the so-called short grasses, which needed less water and put down shallower roots, took hold. The most widespread were grama and buffalo grass, wire grass, little bluestem and bunch grass, and sand grass and sand sage. Grama, for example, usually grows no higher than 12 inches tall; the related buffalo grass grows only half that high. Where slightly more rain fell, the taller wire grass thrived. All of these require thick, tough mats of root systems and tight soil that hold water near the surface.

Bison and antelope were not the only animals of the Great Plains, of course. Pronghorn antelopes, jackrabbits, grasshoppers and locusts, mice, gophers, and prairie dogs all thrived in the semi-arid environment. So did the

By using the bison economically, the Plains tribes ensured that the herd would remain plentiful. The huge expanse of grassland on the Great Plains was the perfect grazing environment for the bison.

creatures who preyed upon them, including moles, snakes, badgers, ferrets, skunks, coyotes, wolves, and raptors such as hawks and eagles. Grassland birds, such as prairie chickens, bobwhites, several species of sparrows, and meadowlarks also flourished.

The first European explorers arrived in the interior of North America in the 16th century. The first to venture into the southern Plains was the Spanish conquistador Francisco Vásquez Coronado, who in 1540 launched an expedition from present-day New Mexico to the

Oklahoma panhandle and northwest to Kansas. The conquistadors had arrived in North America determined to find the legendary "Gran Quivira," a city of enormous wealth with streets paved in gold. For two years, Coronado led his men across hundreds of miles of plains and encountered numerous Southwestern Native American tribes. When the expedition arrived in Kansas, where natives had told them Gran Quivira would be, they found only an ocean of grass unlike anything they'd ever seen. Overwhelmed by the endless grasslands, Coronado wrote bitterly that "not a stone, not a bit of rising ground, not a tree, not a shrub, not anything" seemed to exist there. The only humans they saw were members of the Wichita tribe, living in a few forlorn villages. The Spaniard ended his expedition and returned empty-handed to Mexico, where he had been stationed.

Two centuries later, the Great Plains had changed immensely. Comanches emigrated from Wyoming around 1700. Later the Kiowas came, driven out of their home in the Yellowstone area by the northern Sioux. From the upper Mississippi River, the Cheyenne and Arapaho joined the tribes already settled on the southern Plains. The Plains Indian culture developed into one of the richest and most varied in Native American history.

Some of the most profound changes in the southern Plains occurred as a result of European influence. Native Americans had never seen horses before the Spanish explorers introduced them, but as time passed they began breeding their own. (The Comanches, for example, brought horses that they had stolen from the Apaches, who had raised horses from Spanish runaways or had stolen them from Europeans.) Bison hunts on horseback allowed them to increase their range dramatically and thus kill more animals. Likewise, the Europeans introduced guns—strange contraptions that 16th-century

European settlers intro-
duced the horse and
the gun to the Native
Americans on the Plains.
These tools made hunt-
ing the bison easier, and
the population began to
decline in the 1700s.

Native Americans fearfully described as "canes that spit
fire and made thunder." When Plains Indians themselves
began using guns rather than bows and arrows, bison
hunts became even more deadly. The bison population
began to decline; by the 1700s, about 60 million roamed
the Plains, less than half the number that once did.

It was the arrival of vast waves of white settlers in the
1800s, however—and their conflicts with the Plains
Indians—that not only signaled a profound change in
the lives of Native Americans, but also nearly drove the
bison to extinction. The first American in the southern
Plains was Zebulon Pike, an army lieutenant sent to

explore the region in 1806. Three years earlier, the U.S. government had acquired a huge expanse of land from France. The transaction, called the Louisiana Purchase, doubled the size of the United States. The new territory stretched from the Mississippi River to the Rocky Mountains and from the Gulf of Mexico to British North America.

Pike was unimpressed with the endless sand dunes and grasslands. An anti-expansionist, Pike did not believe that the new country's success depended on its acquiring more land, so he saw what appeared to be a desert as a natural barrier to expansion. "[F]rom these immense prairies may arise one great advantage to the United States," he wrote, "[that is,] the restriction of our population to some certain limits, and thereby a continuation of the union. Our citizens being so prone to . . . extending themselves on the frontiers, will . . . be constrained to limit their extent on the west to the borders of the Missouri and the Mississippi."

Pike was not alone in his opinion: mapmakers began labeling the area the "Great American Desert." Most Americans, however, believed that the unexplored territory beyond the established borders of the United States was theirs for the taking. A Nebraska businessman named Charles Dana Wilber asserted that God had never intended desert land to remain as such. As long as man was "aggressive" in his efforts to tame the land, he asserted, there would be no such thing as desert "anywhere except by man's permission or neglect." Rain would follow the plow, he declared confidently—and most Americans agreed.

The earliest waves of settlers were not farmers, however, but cattlemen from the northwest. While Plains Indians still held their land, ranchers began moving their livestock into the region to take advantage of the enormous expanse of grazing ground. Railroad lines were just beginning to reach the West, so the herds of cattle, averaging about 2,500 head, had to be driven hundred of miles overland to the few established railway connections, such as Abilene and Dodge City. From there the cattle were transported east, where the growing demand for beef was creating huge profits for cattle barons. Among the first ranchers in the region were Oliver Loving and Charles Goodnight, who in 1866 forged a trail from Cheyenne, Wyoming, to central Texas that bypassed the treacherous Comanche and Kiowa territories of the Texas panhandle. The Goodnight-Loving Trail was one of the first cattle trails in the Plains.

As cattle took over the grazing land of the Plains, bison were forced out. The cattlemen held no titles to the land they appropriated; they simply took what they needed. Steer required more grazing land than bison; even so, cattlemen ran up to four times as many cattle to pasture as the grasslands could sustain. Commercial killers began shooting bison to clear grazing land for cattle. Train companies sold ten-dollar tickets giving tourists the opportunity to shoot at the animals from the windows of their luxury coaches as the trains crossed the prairies. Bison-killing contests were held: one Kansas winner killed a record 120 animals in 40 minutes. The famed "Buffalo" Bill Cody, hired to slaughter bison, earned his nickname by killing more than 4,000 of them in two years.

When Plains Indians resisted the takeover of their lands, some federal government officials began to encourage the destruction of bison herds as a means of conquering the Native Americans, whom they viewed as enemies to progress. Texas Congressman James Throckmorton declared, "[I]t would be a great step

Commercial killers began shooting bison to clear land for cattle, devastating the already dwindling population. The most famous of these commercial killers was "Buffalo" Bill Cody, who is said to have killed 4,000 bison in just two years.

forward in the civilization of the Indians and the preservation of peace on the border if there was not a buffalo in existence." With the tacit approval of the U.S. government, military leaders ordered their men to slaughter bison to deprive Native Americans of food. Most of the animals were killed merely for their tongues and hides; their remains were left rotting on the prairies where they fell.

Trappers and traders especially thrived on the booming cattle and bison-killing businesses. By the 1870s they were shipping hundreds of thousands of bison hides annually. In the winter of 1872–73, more than 1.5 million hides reached the cities of the East Coast. By the end of the decade, the once fearsome Plains Indians themselves were defeated, forced off the land that was once their heritage and onto reservations. By 1880, only a few thousand bison remained of the millions of animals that once roamed the Great Plains.

Cattle overgrazing had caused severe depletion of grasslands, which suffered permanent damage. In 1870 a longhorn steer needed about five acres of grass to sustain itself; just 10 years later it required 50 acres. The cattle boom ended after about 20 years, when the exceptionally harsh winter of 1885–86 made grasses even more sparse and left millions of cattle starved and dying.

Farmers, meanwhile, had also begun to make inroads on the Great Plains. In 1862, Congress passed the Homestead Act, granting 160 acres to anyone who settled on the short-grass plains, stayed for at least five years, made "improvements" to the land, and paid a small filing fee. Alternatively, a homesteader could acquire the same amount of land after only six months if he paid $1.25 per acre. As the cattle business died out in the late 1880s, homesteaders began moving into the territory once populated by millions of bison and scores of Native American tribes.

The earliest settlers took the prime land of the river valleys, where water, shelter, and wood were most abundant; later arrivals had to settle for what has since been called "submarginal" land. Most homesteaders didn't have much—one tale describes a family from Kansas who had "nine children and eleven cents"—but when they settled on the Plains they became entrepreneurs. In

general, they were not interested in finding a permanent place to live; they were eager to make money from the land and then move on to a more hospitable place. By 1890, six million people had moved to the Great Plains; in less than a decade the population in the Dust Bowl area doubled.

The homesteaders were nicknamed "sodbusters." Trees were scarce, and the prairie sod they plowed up was so tough that they cut it into blocks and built homes with it. Although the topsoil beneath the sod was rich and

Homesteaders nick-named "sodbusters" used the tough prairie sod to build their homes, like the one seen here.

dark, sodbusters knew only the farming practices that had worked in the East, where the climate was more temperate and rainfall levels were twice that of the Plains. Crops grew well in this soil, but only when the rains came. In 1889, a six-year drought hit the region. Some intact grassland roots prevented the huge dust storms that would later plague the region, but a few areas of the southern Plains were hit harder during this drought than during the Dust Bowl era. Many settlers simply gave up and left. The population of the southern Plains dropped by as much as 90 percent in some counties.

In the early 1900s, the rains arrived once more, and those who had stayed were rewarded with good crop yields. A new farming technique had been developed to prevent the disaster brought on by the recent drought. Called "dry farming," the method required that farmers "deep plow" in the fall, pack the subsoil, stir up the dust as a kind of mulch, and then leave part of their land fallow (tilled but not planted) during the growing season. This, most experts believed, would help restore moisture to the land. Additionally, many farmers began planting grains that were hardier and more drought-resistant than corn, which was the primary crop in the region before the turn of century. Among the new crops were sorghum and a winter wheat known as Turkey Red.

In 1909, at the urging of dry-farming proponents, Congress passed an Enlarged Homestead Act in an effort to revive migration to the Plains. Each settler who moved there now received 320 acres. Once more the Plains were swept with entrepreneurs. These new homesteaders brought another revolution to Great Plains farming: machines. In the interim since the first wave of homesteaders, America had become an industrial nation. Assembly lines turned out not only automobiles, but also tractors and trucks. The powerful new machines allowed farmers not only to increase their production by several times, but also to plant a single crop over a greater area, thereby increasing profits on the land. The grain most often chosen was winter wheat.

In 1912, when Congress reduced the "proving time" for homesteaders from five to three years, land entries soared. Cattle ranchers whose businesses were suffering began selling their acreage to eager settlers. The state of Texas sold farmland for less than 10 percent of the going price in the Midwest. At the same time, the demand for wheat increased as urban areas grew and overseas markets expanded. The real boom in wheat production came when World War I broke out in 1914. Supplies from Russia, the world's largest producer, were cut off, and Europeans—and the rest of the world—turned to the Great Plains farmers.

When the United States entered the war in 1917, the Woodrow Wilson administration encouraged even greater wheat production by passing the Food Control Act, which guaranteed farmers prices of at least $2.00 per bushel of wheat. With the rallying cry, "Plant more wheat! Wheat will win the war!" prices more than doubled in five years. It was a heady time for the Great Plains farmers—the hard times seemed to be gone forever. They believed that they had truly found "wheat heaven."

Trouble
in Wheat
Heaven

The introduction of the steam plow, seen here, and the gas-powered tractor in the early 20th century gave Plains farmers the ability to manage larger tracts of land with less manpower than ever before. Subsequently, the opportunity to profit from farming skyrocketed.

3

In 1919, the wheat farmers of the Great Plains had the highest yields and the greatest profits ever. Seventy-four million acres of wheat—952 million bushels—were produced that year, an increase of almost 40 percent over the years from 1909 to 1913. About a third of it was exported to other countries. In Colorado, Kansas, Nebraska, Oklahoma, and Texas, land planted to wheat increased by more than 13 million acres. Almost 85 percent of the new land was native grassland that had been plowed under.

Unlike earlier sodbusters, the more recent Plains farmers did not require more manpower for larger farmlands. With mechanization, the labor force on the southern Plains actually dropped by one-third, even as the number of farmed acres soared—and the broad, flat Plains themselves made automated plowing, sowing, and harvesting even easier. The earliest machine to reach the Great Plains, around 1900, was the colossal Reeves steam-driven plow, which was so heavy that it severely compressed the earth as it tore up thousands of acres of sod. Less than 20 years later, gas-powered tractors and plows were introduced. Much lighter and less powerful than the steam-driven Reeves, the new machines nevertheless afforded farmers more freedom and control and the opportunity for greater profit than ever before. With a tractor, writer Morrow Mays argued in *Harper's* magazine, the Plains farmer was transformed from "a clod into an operator; from a dumb brute into a mechanic."

Two other machines had a profound effect on the Great Plains. The first was the disc plow. Horse-driven plows of previous decades cut down deep and sliced through grass roots, barely breaking the soil but leaving large lumps of earth that acted as a break for the constant winds. The main feature of the disc plow, aside from its speed, was its series of concave, plate-shaped blades, which were attached vertically to a horizontal bar. When lowered into the soil the blades went shallower than manual plows and broke up clods of topsoil into fine dirt. If fields were disc-plowed often enough, a layer of pulverized dirt settled on the surface. During the period when dry farming was popular, soil experts advised farmers to disc-plow the land as often as possible, especially after rains. It was believed that the layer of dust would help retain moisture. Not until years later did farmers discover how disastrous this advice was.

Wheat production also increased dramatically with the advent of the combined harvester-thresher—commonly called the "combine." At 16 feet wide or more, the machine not only made harvesting more efficient, but it also allowed farmers to do away with nearly all the itinerant laborers they had once required for the job. Now the work of about 20 hired hands could be completed by two or three. As the combine trailed behind a tractor, it cut the wheat and immediately threshed it (separated the seed from the plant). The wheat was then deposited in the bed of a truck that drove aside the combine.

With mechanization, Plains farms were transformed from small, individually owned operations to large-scale enterprises. It was as though a race were being waged to see who could plow up the most acreage and harvest the most grain. During the 1910s and 1920s, even the land that was considered "submarginal"—unsuitable for farming— was plowed and set to wheat wherever possible. "[E]verybody got a John Deere tractor or an old International and really went to plowin' this country and my dad was no different than the rest of 'em," says J.R. Davison, who grew up in the southern Plains. "You know, he'd run that thing all day and when the sun went down, why, he'd come in and do the chores and I'd go runnin' that tractor 'til morning."

Mechanization not only allowed farmers to increase their holdings substantially, but it also meant that they could own land in more than one area. This gave rise to "suitcase farmers"—those who did not live on the land they cultivated. Some were city workers, bankers, and businessmen who traveled to their land, planted the wheat, and then returned to their regular jobs. Others were wheat speculators who took advantage of high prices by paying off the farm almost immediately and then selling it at a profit after one year. The advent of tractors, disc plows, combines, and other farm equipment thus had another unintended effect: it allowed even resident farmers to distance themselves from their livelihoods, to develop an impersonal and predominantly financial relationship with the land.

The "wheat heaven" that Plains farmers thought they

With mechanized farming, a predominantly financial relationship developed between farmers and the land. Farms were bought and sold, and some were abandoned.

had found was beginning to tarnish, however. After World War I ended in November 1918, the foreign demand for wheat dropped considerably as Europeans began returning to their own farms and other supply lines reopened. American wheat prices began dropping in 1920 and remained low. Most Plains farmers had purchased their expensive equipment on credit and were still making payments on it; those who owned their land also had mortgages to pay on their homes, while others were tenants who owed rent to landlords. Farmers were forced to plow up even more land and plant more wheat just to break even—and in their haste to do so, many often abandoned good soil conservation practices.

Trouble was brewing even before the wheat market

began to decline, in part because of poor or careless farming practices. Widespread dry farming and the constant plowing of former grasslands left fewer acres of grazing land for cattle and sheep, while their numbers actually increased. As had happened during the cattle boom of the 19th century, prairie land was overgrazed and most of its resources exhausted. In addition, farmers commonly burned off plant stubble left on the fields after harvests, rather than plowing it under to add nutrients to the soil. The more material they burned off, the fewer nutrients the cropland received and the more depleted it became.

Even worse was the effect of inferior farming practices on the water supplies of the Great Plains. With much of the thick, tough grassland root systems gone from the Plains, the soil was unable to hold the meager amounts of water it received. During years of good rainfall, water "percolates" through healthy prairie land into the subsoil, where it remains in a kind of reservoir underneath the topsoil. When dry spells occur, the root systems of prairie plants rely on this underground moisture for survival. But with the thick, rich sod plowed up and the grasses gone, the subsoil was unable to hold rainwater. Most of the rain that fell during the comparatively "wet" years of the 1920s either evaporated from the surface of the land or was immediately absorbed by the topsoil. When the next dry season hit, nothing would be left.

And bad times were just ahead. On October 29, 1929, the stock market crashed, sending the American economy into a tailspin from which it would not recover for a decade. Thousands of banks closed, and millions watched their life savings disappear. During what is called the Great Depression, many Americans were left completely penniless; they lost their homes and were forced to live on the streets, taking shelter wherever they could find it and relying on charity-sponsored soup kitchens for food. By the spring of 1930, three million men and women were out of work; within the next two years, nine million more would follow. The production of goods and services dropped nearly 30 percent, and even those who kept their jobs were making far less money than they had before the crash. For farmers, this meant that the price of wheat and other produce dropped even more.

On the heels of the Great Depression came another disaster. The eastern United States received very little rainfall during the spring and summer of 1930, and that year a drought spread from Maryland southwest into Missouri and Arkansas. Record low rainfall was recorded in 12 eastern states that year; only Florida received above-normal precipitation. Then the center of the drought moved slowly westward. In the six years between 1931 and 1937, 20 states set records for dryness that have not been matched or exceeded since. By 1932 the dry cycle of the Great Plains had come full circle. Annual rainfall, which already averaged a sparse 20 inches on the southern Plains, shrank to less than half that amount. Within two years, drought had ravaged the Plains from North Dakota to Texas, and from the Mississippi River Valley to the Rocky Mountains.

The most drought-stricken area by far was in the region where the Texas and Oklahoma panhandles border on Kansas, Colorado, and New Mexico. "If one wished to locate the exact center of the dust bowl where the depression was most severely felt, the drought was the most damaging, dust pneumonia cases were most prominent, and wind erosion was most severe," one historian says, "it would be within a triangle running from Pritchett, Colorado, southeast to Boise City, Oklahoma, then northeast through Keyes, Oklahoma [and] Elkhart, Wilburton and Rolla, Kansas, where the third leg of the triangle would turn northwest and return to Pritchett."

This area had enjoyed a bumper wheat crop in 1930. The drought set in only after the crops were well along in the growing cycle. But after harvest, this record crop of wheat sent prices so low that farmers lost money. Many resident farmers were forced by market conditions to seek government aid or find temporary work elsewhere. Suitcase farmers decided not to plant again that year or the next. The result was that in spring 1932, when the lands normally would have been plowed and planted, they lay bare instead. Where crops might have

The stock market crash of October 29, 1929 left the American economy devastated and millions of men and women without jobs. Here, several men eat at a charity run soup kitchen.

stood, tumbleweeds began taking over, snapping off their stems and rolling across the Plains with the wind. In September 1932 a little rain came to the Plains, and farmers held out hope for a fall planting. But it was no use. A drought had arrived and set in. Even those who were receiving government aid found themselves unable to keep up their farms, and many were forced to deed their lands to creditors or were foreclosed on by lending banks. In 1933–34, about one in 10 farms in the Great Plains changed hands. Half of those transactions were involuntary.

And then the heat came. In the summer of 1934, Nebraska recorded a high of 118 degrees Fahrenheit and Iowa reached 115 degrees. Almost 400 people died from a heat wave in Illinois that kept the temperature above 100 degrees for what must have seemed an endless stretch. In 1936 *Newsweek* magazine described the entire United States, seared by drought and baking in the heat, as a "vast simmering cauldron." That year, American farms were losing as much as $25 million in profits each day, and 4,500 people died from heat-related causes.

Most of those who had come to the Plains to make their living farming had arrived during a period of good rainfall, when the soil seemed moist and fertile. They were unaware of the cyclical climate changes and constant winds that could turn the rich farmland of the Great Plains into dust and sand. "The strong south winds that we experience here are our greatest annoyance," wrote the editor of the *Kansas Free State* in Lawrence, Kansas. "They frequently last for several days, and are loaded with the black dust from the burnt prairie, which penetrates every corner of our houses, and makes every one who is exposed to it as 'sooty' as a collier [coal man]." This is a description of the Dust Bowl region—but the editor was writing in 1854.

Although some of the worst dust storms on record would occur during the Dust Bowl period, these were not the first large-scale dusters that area residents faced. The region had suffered dry cycles since the Pleistocene age; they were part of its ecosystem. The first white settlers who arrived in eastern Kansas in the mid-1850s noted the drought conditions and enormous clouds of dirt that blew through the area on the constant Plains winds. The boiling storms were so big that they caused unusual weather hundreds of miles away. In Ohio, a professor at Oberlin

By 1932 a drought had set in on the Great Plains. Combined with the excessive heat that characterized the next few summers, once fertile soil became barren tracts of dust and sand.

College recorded "black snow" in February 1855. In April 1860, Fort Scott, Kansas, experienced one of the worst dust storms ever recorded there; two days later, black rain fell on Syracuse, New York.

It is clear from these accounts and others from the late 19th century that the huge dust storms (also called "dusters" or "rollers") that most people have come to associate with the 1930s occurred naturally on the Great Plains long before the Dust Bowl era. During each dry weather cycle, the southern Plains in particular were subject to periods of drought and extensive wind erosion. Most people believe that human misuse of the land in the early 1900s was solely to blame for the severe conditions in the 1930s, but it was only one of many factors that led to the Dust Bowl. "Without doubt the plowed soil added to the intensity of the storms [in the 1930s]," says a leading historian, "but it did not cause dust storms."

Nevertheless, the dust storms that began scouring the Great Plains during the 1930s were so destructive and so violent that they left residents reeling. In 1933, weather observers in the Texas and Oklahoma panhandles reported between 70 and 140 dust storms. In November 1933 an enormous dust storm that originated in the northern Plains states dropped tons of dirt on East Coast towns from New York to Georgia. The Weather Bureau dubbed this event "the first great storm." Two more storms that began in North or South Dakota blew eastward, and then another enormous and violent duster, lasting from May 9–12, 1934, struck the country. On May 11 alone, 300 million tons of topsoil in the southern Plains region were blown away on the high prairie winds. The legendary duster on April 14, 1935 affected states from the Dakotas to Florida. The enormous, boiling dust clouds traveled as far east as the Atlantic Ocean, where ships found mysterious layers of silt on their decks.

The drought that began in earnest in 1932 and the frequent, large dust storms that began blowing through the Great Plains in early 1933 were among several weather phenomena that caused concern. During that period, the area that would later become known as the Dust Bowl suffered other extreme weather: blizzards, tornadoes, torrential rains and flash floods, and tremendous thunderstorms that carried hail all plagued the region. The droughts and dust storms soon became the biggest concerns, however, at least for residents of the five-state area around the Texas and Oklahoma panhandles. They would suffer another two years of unrelenting dust before federal government officials in Washington began to understand the seriousness of the situation.

The droughts, heat waves, and dust storms of the 1930s hit the Great Plains at the worst possible time—during the Great Depression that raged through the country, and just after a period of expansion that had increased America's farmland by millions of acres. Without the economic crash, what would have been considered a normal or perhaps slightly worse than average dry spell in the Great Plains became the greatest agricultural disaster the United States had ever seen.

A young boy shields his nose and mouth against the blowing sands of a dust storm. Residents of the Dust Bowl would have to learn to adapt to the frequent blinding storms in order to survive.

Mean Skies and Hard Times

R obert Geiger, a journalist for the *Washington Evening Star,* was in Guymon, Oklahoma, on Black Sunday, April 14, 1935. In an article he filed about the storm, he gave the region the nickname that still stands today. "Three little words," he wrote, "achingly familiar on a western farmer's tongue, rule life in the dust bowl of the continent: If it rains." Soon even the area's residents were calling their home the "Dust Bowl."

What was it like to live during the Dust Bowl period? What happened during a roller, as residents called the huge dust storms? Caroline Henderson lived on a farm near Shelton, Oklahoma, with her husband. "There are days," she wrote a friend, "when for hours at a time we cannot see the windmill fifty feet from the kitchen door."

Two types of dust storms plagued the Great Plains during the 1930s. "Sand blows" were frequent occurrences caused by the constant southwest winds that blew across the Great Plains. Sandy, heavier soil was picked up by these low winds and drifted into dunes along fence posts, ditches, and buildings. The second kind of storm, the ominous "black blizzards," were the result of cold air masses from the north generating static electricity that lifted the silty, lighter soil into the atmosphere. The blizzards rolled in like huge, boiling waves up to 8,000 feet high. Sometimes they brought thunder and lightning as well, but perhaps the most frightening dust blizzards were the ones that blew in with a terrifying silence. Residents knew they were coming because the temperature would drop sharply— sometimes as much as 50 degrees in a few hours. They might see flocks of birds or herds of jackrabbits racing before the coming storm, the birds chattering nervously and settling in yards or roadways. And then on the horizon, a wall of blackness like a tidal wave would appear. Those caught outside in the rollers stood a very real risk of dying before they reached their destination. Most times, residents could not see their own hands held up before their faces.

Once the storms ended, the dust and dirt that remained was an affliction in itself. Kansas resident Judge Cowen recalls:

> The farmhouses looked terrible—the dust was deposited clear up to the window sills in these farmhouses, clear up to the window sills. And even about half of the front door was blocked by this sand. And if people inside wanted to get out, they had to climb out through the window to get out with a shovel to shovel out the front door. And, ah, there was no longer any yard at all there, not a green sprig, not a living thing of any kind, not even a field mouse. Nothing.

While the men and boys took the risk of being out in farm fields or on the roads when dust storms

blew through, women and girls were usually responsible for maintaining the home. During the Dust Bowl, the burden of housekeeping was exceptionally heavy. "Women checked to make sure the rags and gummed tape stuffed under doorsills and on window ledges were still snug and blocking out the breeze. They replaced bedsheets suspended from the ceilings to trap floating dirt." A house sealed tightly enough to keep out most of the dirt would eventually run out of oxygen, however, and those inside would have to open a window. Keeping a home in order became endless drudgery; even tasks one would usually

The fierce winds of a "roller" would deposit sand in drifts that covered windows and doors. This tiny farmhouse on the Plains is almost completely engulfed in a sand bank.

tackle only once or twice a year, such as sweeping the attic, had to be attended to far more frequently. Some learned their lessons the hard way—the weight of accumulated dust in attics made ceilings sag or collapse.

Ann Marie Low, who lived on a farm in North Dakota during the Dust Bowl, kept a diary of those years in which she describes an average day of work with her mother:

> Mama couldn't make bread until I carried water to wash the bread mixer. I couldn't churn until the churn was washed and scalded. We just couldn't do anything unless something was washed first. Laundry day was especially demanding. I had to wash out the boiler, wash tubs, and the washing machine before we could use them. Then every towel, piece of bedding, and garment had to be taken out doors to have as much dust as possible shaken out before washing.

The Low family was among many residents forced to deal somehow with the tremendous amount of dust that hung in the air and drove through in storms—without the benefit of electric washing machines, running water, or, in some cases, indoor bathrooms. One farm woman recalled the elaborate rituals she developed when she heard the wind pick up: "I went back into the house, hastily covered the table with newspapers and an old cloth, covered the water pail, covered all the unwashed cooking utensils, made my bed and spread an old denim comfort over it. . . . Next I put on an old stocking cap to protect my hair, and old jacket to comfort my shaking body, and sat down by the kitchen range with my feet on the oven door. The room soon filled with a dust haze through which the coal-oil lamp made a pale light."

Living with the constant threat of violent dust storms took an emotional toll on farm families. Melt White struggles to describe the extreme dust during the spring of 1935: "The wind blew 27 days and nights without quittin', and I remember that's why my mother just—I thought she was going to go crazy because it was just—it was—you got desperate, because if the wind blew durin' the day or durin' the night and let up, you got some relief. But just day and night, 24 hours, one 24-hour [period] after the other, it just—but it's 27 days and nights in the spring of 1935 it didn't let up."

It was difficult to sleep under such conditions. Dust Bowl residents had to cover their noses and mouths with wet rags while they slept. They covered the cribs of infants with cloths, and anxious parents tossed in their beds fearing that their babies might breathe in so much dust while sleeping that they would suffocate. People learned not to move around much in their sleep; that way they wouldn't disturb the dust that settled on their blankets and brought on coughing bouts if they shifted.

Humans were not the only creatures suffering from the dust. Part of every family's daily chores was to check on the farm animals at dawn to make sure they hadn't suffocated overnight. The violent storms could bury chickens, pigs, and dogs—sometimes even cattle. Children cleared caked dust from the nostrils of the cows several times a day.

In these conditions, it was impossible to eat food without also eating dirt. T.H. Watkins, an historian of the Great Depression, describes how most Plains families avoided eating too much of the blowing dust: "Women learned to put up water and milk in tightly sealed Mason jars at the first sign of a storm so that the liquids would not become an undrinkable sludge. . . . Bread could be kneaded in a dresser drawer covered with a cloth into which two holes had been cut so the breadmaker's hands could do the work. . . . Everything was eaten the instant it

Farm animals often suffocated to death in the dust storms, and children had to clear the caked dust from the nostrils of the cattle. Here, a herd of cows huddles together for protection against a storm.

left the stove in the few precious moments before grime covered it. Even so, dust was ingested like a condiment with every meal." Another historian recalls a farmer in Griggs, Oklahoma, whose wife set out each meal under a tablecloth. When the family came to the table and finished saying grace, each person would raise a corner of the tablecloth and put his or her head underneath to eat.

Ingesting dust with food was bad enough, but breathing it was dangerous. The symptoms of an ailment called dust pneumonia had medical professionals debating whether a new strain of disease had developed. Whether or not that was true, the number of asthma, bronchitis, and tuberculosis cases soared in the heart of the Dust Bowl during the worst years of the drought. Silicosis, a serious lung condition caused by inhaling silica (an element found in quartz and sand), was another hazard. Each major dust storm would bring newspaper reports of additional deaths from breathing the dust.

The Plains had experienced dust storms before, but rarely on the scale or frequency of the 1930s. Strange phenomena resulted from the black blizzards. Billions of dirt particles rubbing against each other produced static electricity that would jolt anyone who touched a metal object. Harley Holladay and Art Leonard, two Dust Bowl survivors from Dodge City, Kansas, remembered their bizarre experiences of Black Sunday:

> [Harley] turned back to the house, but now the sky was almost coal black. He was only a few feet from the porch yet had to fall to his hands and knees and crawl before he could find the house. . . .
>
> Art Leonard, on his way to work, had to inch his way to his father's store. Drivers stuck in the storm put on their headlights, but it didn't do much good. Neighbors out for a Sunday drive crashed into one another. Drivers had another problem, too. The static electricity . . . shorted out ignitions. It also jammed radio broadcasts and created an eerie outline along the metal edges of windmill blades and fences. When he looked out the window Harley was struck by what he saw—balls of electricity dancing along the barbed wire.

Another survivor, Gordon Grice, remembers sitting in the well house with his family through one big storm. "Suddenly the lamp went out. Gordon reached in his pocket, retrieved a match, lit it, and watched in amazement as the thickly settling dust buried the flame from the match."

As if the record heat, terrible droughts, and flying dirt weren't difficult enough for farming families to deal with, they were also beset with giant clouds of grasshoppers, which thrive in hot, dry weather. The swarms of insects that migrated across the stricken farmlands were so thick during the worst years of the drought (from 1932 to 1935) that they sometimes blotted out the sun. A South Dakota resident later remembered a seemingly biblical plague: "Migrating hordes of grasshoppers descended so thick you couldn't see the sides of buildings. Fence posts were twice their normal size with grasshoppers, and highways were slushy and slick. As soon as [the insects] hit the ground they headed for the tree and started up it and began to eat the leaves. The next morning they had eaten every leaf, and there were a lot of hoppers eating the young branches. It didn't take very long and they killed the tree." When locust and grasshopper swarms weren't afflicting Great Plains farmers, jackrabbits were. Some areas even suffered plagues of spiders. In Morton and Stevens counties in Kansas in August 1934, several people became seriously ill and one boy died from black widow spider bites.

Unlike thunderstorms, dust storms could last for hours, sometimes days or even months. During one siege that lasted 60 days, Vi Kraft of Hooker, Oklahoma, remembers townswomen rushing to hang out their clean laundry when the wind lifted enough to see just a block away. In Eva, another Oklahoma town, a man named Cecil Grable was trapped at his gas station for several days, unable to see across the street. In its April 22, 1935 issue, eight days after Black Sunday, *TIME* magazine described the storms that were so widespread and so

In addition to the excessive heat and drought, swarms of grasshoppers also plagued the Plains farmers. Here a man is seen trying to peer out a window covered in grasshoppers.

severe that they were no longer merely the problem of Plains farmers:

Last week farmers in ten Midwestern States had sand in their beards, in their hair, in their ears, in their eyes, in their mouths, in their pockets, in their pants, in their boots, in their milk, coffee, soup and stew. Dust poured through the cracks in farmhouse walls, under the doors, down the chimneys. In northwest Oklahoma a hundred families fled their homes. Every school in Baca County, Colorado was closed. In Texas the windswept hayfields were alive with blinded sparrows. Methodist congregations in Guymon, Oklahoma met three times a day to pray for rain. Originally confined to a 200-mile strip between Canada and Mexico, last week's dust storm suddenly swirled eastward over Missouri, Iowa and Arkansas, crossed the Mississippi to unload on Illinois, Indiana, Kentucky, Tennessee and Louisiana. With half the nation blanketed in silt, farmers everywhere were asking what was going to happen to the wheat crop.

Forced to adjust to a life of constant dust, some families discovered a new pastime—after an exceptionally big storm, they might pack picnic lunches and spend time in the fields searching for long-buried Native American arrowheads uncovered by severe soil erosion. Even during the worst periods, people kept a sense of humor. Postcards showing enormous grasshoppers stopping train engines or pulling a plow gave sufferers of the dust plague a chuckle when they needed one. Two weeks before Black Sunday, *TIME* magazine observed that "An Oklahoman was said to have fainted when a drop of rain fell on his head, to have been revived only when two buckets of sand were thrown in his face."

Other Dust Bowl jokes abounded: a tourist saw a perfectly good 10-gallon hat lying by the side of the road. When he stopped to pick it up, he was shocked to find a head underneath it. "Can I help you?" the surprised tourist asked. "No, I'm fine," the farmer responded. "At least let me give you a ride into town," the tourist insisted. "That won't be necessary," the farmer answered. "I'm on a horse." Margaret Bourke-White, a photographer who traveled mostly by air throughout the Dust Bowl to document the damage, heard a tall tale about a pilot who had engine trouble during a Plains dust storm. He put on

Pilots like Margaret Bourke-White, seen here, flew over the Dust Bowl to assess the damage.

a parachute and jumped—and it took him six hours to shovel his way to the ground.

While jokes and stories helped, the economic realities of living in the Dust Bowl were nevertheless painful. Nearly one-third of all Americans lived on farms in the early 1930s. In 1932–33, 12 million Americans were unemployed. Without regular incomes, they were unable to buy even staple goods, including the foods produced on U.S. farms. One difference between the non-rural unemployed who suffered the ravages of economic depression and the farmers of the Great Plains was that the farmers had to keep working, even if they couldn't make any money doing so. *TIME* magazine's April 22, 1935 issue included grim statistics about the year's crops:

> U.S. farmers had planted 44,306,000 acres in winter wheat last autumn. Drought and dust had forced them to abandon 12,405,000 acres. The wheat standing on the remaining 31,901,000 acres on April 1 was estimated to yield 435,499,000 bushels—69% of normal. West of the [Mississippi] river . . . more than 40% of the winter wheat seeded last autumn was expected to fail. Hardest hit was Kansas where rainfall in March was only 56% of normal and the crop 47% of normal. Last week six Kansas counties reported their wheat crop a total failure.

How did people manage to get by during the worst widespread drought and the most severe economic depression in American history? A few bright moments shone through the grim 1930s. Even during the worst years, enough rain fell in the Dust Bowl that a few scant crops survived, and those meager successes buoyed the hopes of nearby farmers. Oklahoma resident Edna Barnes remembers that in some years her father's crops failed completely, but there was always a neighbor nearby who had managed to raise enough of a crop to encourage them not to give up.

Unlike unemployed urban Americans, however, farmers were at least able to raise a little food for their own families. Although few kitchen gardens survived the dust storms, jackrabbits, and grasshopper plagues, enterprising farm women found ways to avoid starvation. Rita Van Amber, author of the book *Stories and Recipes of the Great Depression of the 1930s*, says that her mother canned and preserved wild grasses and weeds, such as dandelion, cowslip greens, and lamb's-quarters; she would then prepare and serve them as she would vegetables.

Resourceful Plains residents found other ways to get through tough times. Historian Paul Bonnifield, author of the book *The Dust Bowl: Men, Dirt, and Depression*, records that an Oklahoman farmer "traded his work team for a pair of greyhounds and spent most of the hard years hunting rabbits." The man not only helped rid the region of the pests, but he also provided meat for his family and traded some rabbits for other goods. The animals that the family didn't eat or trade were sold for their fur and for animal feed.

Early in the "Dirty Thirties," during the wheat glut just before the most severe period of depression and drought, farmers were also urged to feed some of their harvests to their livestock rather than sell it. As a result, farmers had more chickens, milk cows, and hogs than they'd ever kept before. They sold eggs, milk, and cream to raise money, and were able to keep the hogs by feeding them skimmed milk from the dairy cows. This tided them over through the lean years—at least until they were forced to sell their cows (and the hogs, which had fed on the milk).

Farmers were not the only Plains residents who suffered, of course. When railroad worker Len Cloninger was laid off by the Rock Island Railroad, he got his hands on an old truck and started hauling discarded cattle from the drought region into Arkansas. There, he traded them for canned blackberries, which he in turn traded for money and staples. Like a few other men, George Devers became a jack-of-all-trades, hiring himself out to any ranch that would take him to do any job they asked.

Abiding by the old saying, "Use it up, wear it out, make it do, or do without" helped other families keep going as well. Food was never wasted, of course, but Plains people discovered other ways of tightening belts.

The combination of the Dust Bowl and the Great Depression left many Plains farmers extremely poor. They had to be frugal with the supplies they had, and recycle whenever they could. Here, a mother wears a pair of pants she has fashioned from a potato sack.

Edna Barnes's family simply closed off most of the house to keep the fuel bills low. School-aged children each had two outfits; they wore the best of them to school and the other at home. Some folks had always had a little extra income, even before the Dust Bowl. "Moonshine"—homemade alcohol—had been produced in the region for decades. Its heyday, not surprisingly, came during Prohibition, the period from 1920 to 1933 when alcohol was outlawed in the United States. Local lawmen usually turned a blind eye toward moonshining, reasoning that it was another way for townspeople to take in a few dollars. Nor were most families concerned about the lawbreaking activities. "The wives of moonshiners said nothing . . . because it brought in a little extra cash,'" says Bonnifield. "And, most of the raw material for the liquor [usually distilled from corn] was raised at home, which kept expenses to a minimum."

The cattlemen who toughed it out during the Dust Bowl were equally inventive: they gathered soapweed and used it for livestock feed, either by chopping up the coarse plants themselves or having it milled. In New Mexico, cattlemen torched off the spines of prickly pear plants and allowed the cattle to feed off the now-smooth vegetation. Even tumbleweeds were fed to cattle.

Despite all the ways Plains families found to marshal their resources, and despite their courageous efforts to hold onto their land and homes, thousands of people from the drought-stricken Dust Bowl found themselves completely broke, at times verging on starvation. These residents had little or no choice but to pack up their belongings and leave, heading West for what they hoped was a better life. And no matter what state these migrants came from, they would eventually become known disparagingly as "Okies."

When the farming mecha-
nization of the 1920s made
tools like this plow obsolete,
many farmhands lost their
jobs. They were forced to
migrate out of region to
look for work in other
areas. A large portion of
the migrants came from
Oklahoma, and subse-
quently all migrants came
to be known as "Okies."

The Okie Migration

5

Lots of folks back East they say, leaving home every day
Beating the hot old dusty way to the California line
Cross the desert sands they roll, getting out of the old Dust Bowl
Think they're going to a sugar bowl, but here's what they find
Now police at the port of entry say,
"You're number fourteen thousand for today."

Oh, if you ain't got the do re mi, folks, you ain't got the do re mi
Why you better get back to beautiful Texas, Oklahoma, Georgia, Kansas, Tennessee
California is a garden of Eden, a paradise to live in or see
But believe it or not, you won't find it so hot
If you ain't got the do re mi.

—lyrics to "Do Re Mi" by Woody Guthrie, 1937

The desperate straits of residents in the Dust Bowl region were certainly intensified by wind and soil erosion from the dust storms, the droughts of 1931–1937, the plagues of grasshoppers and jackrabbits, and the Great Depression. But the main source of the grinding poverty that drove hundreds of thousands of people to abandon their land in the Midwest and southern Plains was the farming mechanization that began during the 1920s.

When the tractor, combine, and disc plow came into widespread use, Plains farmers enlarged their lands but needed fewer hired hands. Many workers lost their jobs and were forced to move elsewhere. By the time the stock market crashed in 1929, the Great Plains were already experiencing what is called an "out-migration"—residents leaving the area to find work in another region.

But the Great Depression undoubtedly affected the unfortunate people who were forced out of the Dust Bowl. During this period it was almost impossible to find other work. Landowners and farmers who had gone deeply in debt to buy automated farm equipment were now unable to repay what they had borrowed. When a farmer fell too far behind in his mortgage or loan payments, the lender (usually a bank) foreclosed—took possession of the farm—and sold it at auction to pay off the debt. Sometimes foreclosers would bulldoze buildings on the land they were selling, giving rise to the term "tractored out" to describe those who were expelled. As the number of foreclosures increased, bands of farmers, angry about this threat to their livelihood, often launched "penny auctions." They appeared at foreclosure auctions to intimidate possible bidders, and when they succeeded, they would bid a few cents for the equipment and

property that was on the block. Because no one else dared to bid, the farmers won the auctions—and then returned everything to its original owner.

The Dust Bowl wasn't the only region where tenant farmers and laborers were having trouble making ends meet, of course. Even though newspaper reports, famous photographs, folk songs, and books describe the great "Dust Bowl migration," the majority

Many banks foreclosed on farms like this one when the owners fell too far behind on their mortgage payments. The farms were then sold at auction to the highest bidder.

of 1930s migrants didn't come from the Texas and Oklahoma panhandle area that is considered the heart of the Dust Bowl. Many historians point out that the Dust Bowl was only part of a vast region affected by that decade's droughts, and that the so-called Okies usually "came neither from the dust bowl nor from the areas of worst distress in the drought region." Instead, most of the westward migrants of the 1930s were from eastern Oklahoma, Arkansas, Missouri, and Texas, areas that were affected by drought and economic hard times but were not considered part of the Dust Bowl.

Great numbers of people had been leaving the farms of the semi-arid Great Plains since the 1920s. More often, the migrants came from farms in the humid southeastern states. Because America was enjoying a period of prosperity, however, few people noticed the migration. When the droughts began spreading and the spectacular, deadly dust storms began to blow, politicians and reporters could not help but notice what was happening in the Midwest. Most simply assumed that it was the dust storms and drought of the southern Plains that were causing the growing westward migration.

Nobody knows how many people migrated in the U.S. during the Depression and drought years. Most historians believe than less than a quarter of the Dust Bowl's population left their farms. Even so, communities were disrupted across the Plains states. "We hated to see anyone leave," remembers Imogene Glover, a resident. "There were so few close neighbors or close friends or relatives. And we hated for 'em to leave." "Lots of people left," Lorene White recalls of the town where she lived. "The family west

(continued on page 72)

"BREATHE A POUND OF DUST": WOODY GUTHRIE'S MUSIC

On the 14th day of April of 1935,
There struck the worst of dust storms that ever filled the sky.
You could see that dust storm comin', the cloud looked deathlike black,
And through our mighty nation, it left a dreadful track.

From Oklahoma City to the Arizona line,
Dakota and Nebraska to the lazy Rio Grande,
It fell across our city like a curtain of black rolled down,
We thought it was our judgement, we thought it was our doom.

Born on July 14th, 1912 in Okemah, Oklahoma, Woodrow Wilson Guthrie was virtually homeless by the time he was 14. After his family broke up that year, he began wandering the country practicing his newfound hobby—folk singing. In 1937 he landed a job singing for a Los Angeles radio station. Soon after, while he was in New York City, his music was discovered by Alan Lomax, assistant director of the Archive of Folk Songs at the Library of Congress. Lomax persuaded Guthrie to record his original songs for the Library of Congress, and he was so impressed by Guthrie's music that he convinced several record companies to produce his albums. One of the most important of these was Guthrie's six-album set, *Dust Bowl Ballads*.

Guthrie's music was not commercially successful in his day, but his songs painted vivid pictures of life in the Dust Bowl and in the migrant camps of California. Still, he thought of himself as merely a scribe, documenting the lives and words of the people themselves. A regular columnist for the *Daily Worker*, Guthrie explained the inspiration behind his folk songs: "[The *Dust Bowl Ballads*] came out of the hearts and mouths of the Okies," he wrote. "On no occasion have I referred to myself as either an entertainer or a singer and I'd better not start now."

Before his death in 1967, Guthrie wrote and composed more than 1,000 folk songs, most depicting in colorful language the worries, joys, and sorrows of working-class Americans. Although many other singers and musicians recorded tales of living through the Great Depression and the Dust Bowl, Guthrie's work, still popular today, has earned him a place as perhaps the greatest folk musician in American history.

(continued from page 70)

of us left, and they had kids that we played with. Ah, there was a family, two families, east of us, that left."

Still, the numbers of those who did leave the region are staggering. In the 1930s, especially after 1935, about 2.5 million people left the Plains states. Oklahoma lost 440,000 people—almost 19 percent of its population—and Kansas lost 227,000. More than 300,000 of them headed for California, and the Pacific Northwest (Oregon and Washington) gained about 460,000 people. These migrants, who sought to make their living working as pickers, boxers, or balers on produce farms, were memorialized in the Joad family, the main characters in John Steinbeck's 1939 Pulitzer Prize–winning novel *The Grapes of Wrath*:

> The dispossessed were drawn west from Kansas, Oklahoma, Texas, New Mexico; from Nevada and Arkansas, families, tribes, dusted out, tractored out. Carloads, caravans, homeless and hungry; twenty thousand and fifty thousand and a hundred thousand and two hundred thousand. They streamed over the mountains, hungry and restless—restless as ants, scurrying to find work to do—to lift, to push, to pull, to pick, to cut—anything, any burden to bear, for food. The kids are hungry. We got no place to live. Like ants scurrying for work, for food, and most of all for land.

The Okies—wherever their origin—sold everything they could to raise money for an old truck or jalopy. They packed what they had left, tied down bed mattresses, chairs, and other large possessions to the roofs or sides of the vehicles, and drove westward. Those who couldn't afford a car or truck

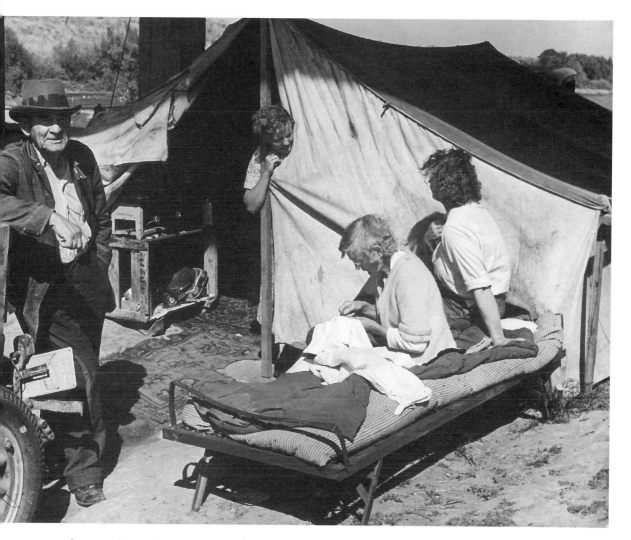

hopped on freight trains and rode the rails. Contrary to legend, most of the migrants did not move as far as California. Many simply moved to the next county. A great number of the migrants who did cross state lines usually went to a contiguous state, such as Texas or New Mexico, to regions that were unaffected by the drought. Still, the waves of migrants to California during the 1930s were enormous: according to one estimate, it was the destination for 40 percent of all migrants who crossed state lines

In his book *The Grapes of Wrath*, John Steinbeck memorialized the plight of the Okies by following the struggles of the fictional Joad family. Steinbeck interviewed many Okies to ensure that his book would give an accurate representation of their hardships.

Okies sold most of their possessions to buy run-down cars called jalopies, which they packed with any of the household items they didn't sell and drove to the promise of a better life.

during the second half of the decade. California's population during this period increased by 20 percent over its 1930 number.

Those who did drive all the way to California embarked on a trip that they believed would take them to the "promised land." They had heard from relatives and friends who had gone before them, or from handbills distributed in the Dust Bowl by big California growers, that the state was a region of fertile valleys where farmers raised vast fields of lettuce and cotton, cultivated orchards of plums, nectarines, peaches, and walnuts, and established huge grape vineyards. Hundreds of thousands of Okies began the long trek westward—usually along Route 66, the "Mother Road"—hoping to find a new start in California. All it took to get started was about 10 dollars for gasoline and a little food. The trip might last from a few weeks to six months: they had to stop and work along the way to buy more food, water, and gasoline. "They might pick cotton in Twitty, Texas, to earn enough money to get to Wikieup, Arizona, in time for the lettuce and carrot harvest," one author explains. If the trip came to a halt because of a car or truck breakdown, the driver would hitch a ride into the next town and find some way to make a little money. Even 50 cents or a dollar would buy gas or a spare part to keep the family going another day.

The migrants crossed the Black Mountains on narrow, winding roads at the edge of cliffs, in their unreliable cars and trucks, weighed down with furniture and even stoves. If they made it that far, the Mojave Desert awaited them—143 miles of mostly uninhabited land with few gas stations and even less water. Temperatures often reached 120 degrees, and though some were used to the intense heat that baked the Plains during the droughts, they were unaccustomed to the desert. Ralph Richardson, a gas station owner in New Mexico, feared that the migrants' inexperience could cost them their lives. He posted a sign on a cholla (a species of cactus) that read, "CARRY WATER OR THIS IS WHAT YOU WILL LOOK LIKE." Richardson knew the migrants were desperate—and often heartbreakingly poor. "They even offered to leave the [family] dog, the cat, and the canary for gas. Frightened, those people were frightened, and they came through here thinking they were headed for the promised land. . . . I warned them about those ideas, but they went on," Richardson remembers.

What the migrants hoped to find in the Golden State of California and what they actually found, however, were very different. They had almost no hope of owning their own farms in the vast, company-controlled farmlands of California, where less than 10 percent of the farms produced more than half of the state's crops. Most migrants ended up in large cities such as Los Angeles, San Diego, and San Francisco, but some kept to the work they knew best: farming. These migrant workers moved with the harvest, 500 miles a year on average, working long hours at backbreaking tasks. They were paid just pennies a day.

The Okies often lived in shabby "ditch camps" or shantytowns, in improvised shelters made of cardboard, scrap wood or metal, or bedsheets. Ditch camps had no toilets, running water, or electricity. Dysentery, pneumonia, and tuberculosis ran rampant, as did other diseases caused by nutritional deficiency, such as pellagra and rickets. A California relief worker described one dilapidated camp: "The outside appearance of most dwellings is repellant. Decay has rotted scrap construction material and the overflow piles of sodden junk help prepare the visitor for a sordid look within the household. Even in mid-day the interior is dark, but the noxious odors are strong of dampness, rot, stale atmosphere."

The migrants faced another adversity as well: no one wanted them there. Poor, often uneducated, desperate, and wearing threadbare clothing, they

were greeted with disdain and called "dumb Okies." For two months in 1935, Los Angeles police were stationed at the largest entry points in the state to turn migrants away if they had no money or proof of a job waiting for them. This illegal action was eventually stopped by the state attorney general and the American Civil Liberties Union.

Large farm owners welcomed the influx of new laborers, however, at least at harvest time. The thousands of Mexican and Asian migrant workers

When the Okies arrived in California, they found that the promised land they expected was not waiting for them. They could not afford their own farms, and were forced to live in shanty-towns like the one seen here, where living conditions were deplorable.

in California had begun forming labor unions; for example, cotton-pickers staged a widespread strike in 1933. But the thousands of Okies entering the state allowed growers to keep wages low and still retain workers. Competition for jobs was fierce.

Okies faced a level of prejudice that African Americans, Mexican Americans, and Asian Americans had been facing for decades. "The Okies," said one California resident, were "shiftless trash who lived like hogs." During an age when segregation of whites and blacks was the norm, one theater in the San Joaquin Valley posted a sign that read, "Negroes and Okies upstairs." H.L. Mencken, a well-known author and journalist, held an appallingly hateful opinion of the Okies: "They are simply, by God's inscrutable will, inferior men," he wrote in his newspaper, the *American Mercury,* in 1936, "and inferior they will remain until, by a stupendous miracle, he gives them equality among his angels." Mencken's solution: move them out of the Plains, away from America's farmlands, and pay them to be sterilized so that they could not produce offspring.

Starvation was a very real possibility for these unfortunate people. The fertile farms of California usually produced surplus goods, more than could be harvested or sold—but the Okies dared not help themselves to it. If they did, the growers destroyed the produce by pouring oil on it and setting it on fire. They believed this would force the Okies to move on. John Steinbeck witnessed this and called it the "saddest, bitterest thing of all," a crime, he declared, "that goes beyond denunciation."

Although the state of California had an extensive relief network in place, one had to have lived in the state for a year to be eligible for relief. This left out

most of the migrants who desperately needed help. In 1935, the federal government began building cleaner and better camps for migrants, and by 1937, 10 federal camps operated in the San Joaquin Valley, with showers, bathrooms, and small houses available at very low rent. If families couldn't afford even this amount, they were assigned odd jobs around the camp to earn their keep. The camps also had community buildings such as auditoriums and recreation

The federal government responded to the influx of migrants into California by building camps designed to provide Okies with better living conditions. By 1937 most migrants could find small houses in camps with showers and toilets.

halls. By 1941, 45,000 migrants lived in 13 permanent camps and six mobile ones established by the U.S. government. The new camps not only helped migrants remain healthy, but they also gave them a sense of dignity, community, and hope—a sorely needed commodity.

But prejudice dies hard. Even though the Okies were victims of the economic and environmental forces beyond their control, signs all over California read: "Okies—Go Shopping Somewhere Else," or "Okies Go Home!" One California woman wrote to President Franklin D. Roosevelt protesting the presence of Okies near her home:

> A Federal migratory camp is being established adjacent to my property at Porterville, Tulare County, California. Knowing the character of migrants from my experience in dealing with them, I object to these hordes of degenerates being located at my very door. These "sharecroppers" are not a noble people looking for a home and seeking an education for their children. They are unprincipled degenerates looking for something for nothing. The fact that they are leaving their native land unfit for human habitation is not surprising. Their ignorance and maliciousness in caring for trees, crops, vines, and the land is such that California will be ruined if farming is left to them. Please do not put these vile people at my door to depreciate my property and to loot my ranch.

In spite of the grinding poverty, the disease-ridden living conditions, the near-starvation levels of food, and the hatred and contempt they endured, the Okies were in California to stay. Even if they wanted to leave, they did not have the means to do so. "I've made my mistake," one farmer-turned-migrant told his homesick wife, "and now we can't go back. I've got nothing to farm with." For those back home who were fortunate enough to keep their farms during the Dust Bowl, however, the tide was about to turn: in the mid- to late 1930s, they would be offered a New Deal.

It was President Franklin D. Roosevelt's belief that the federal government had the duty to help Americans weather bad times. During the New Deal era, FDR created programs designed to help Dust Bowl farmers survive financially, and to repair the land that was destroyed by drought, heat, and over-farming.

A New Deal for the Dust Bowl

Federal government relief efforts for the Dust Bowl began with the Agricultural Adjustment Act, which was passed in 1933. The act created the Agricultural Adjustment Administration, or AAA, whose purpose was to create a "scarcity" of grain and cotton crops that would drive prices back up and aid Midwestern farmers.

Officials in the AAA and in other federal agencies concerned with agriculture, such as the Interior Department, interpreted their duties to include long-term planning for land usage. They believed that the best way to solve the problem in the semi-arid Plains was to return much of the cultivated land to grassland. Ideally, in the eyes of the AAA, wheatlands in the Dust Bowl would be replaced either by cattle ranches or by natural, undisturbed prairie.

Agents also believed that increasing the size of individual farms in the Dust Bowl would increase their economic usefulness. In a wrongheaded attempt to aid Plains farmers, they aimed to give financial aid to those who were successful at farming, so that they could buy or lease neighboring land. Of course, this required that those less successful be removed from their own land to make it available for sale or rent. But the federal government did not take this into account, and made no concessions for those who would be displaced. These farmers had no choice but to migrate. Moreover, the credit that the government provided for farmers to increase their acreage was meager. As a result of this program, one farmer might be forced from the land, but another farmer could not afford to purchase it. Only the government itself, it turned out, could afford to buy Dust Bowl land.

Even worse, the Interior Department helped the AAA with its policy goals by lending money to cattle farmers in the Dust Bowl heartland—but not to wheat farmers. And despite the recommendations of some agencies that farmers be subsidized for expanding their farms, the government aimed to "re-grass" the heart of the Dust Bowl and return it to federally owned property. Clearly, the plan was at odds with the idea of helping small farmers expand.

Ironically, the AAA began reducing the nation's surplus of wheat, cotton, and other products by allocating payments to farmers who *stopped* growing these crops. The payment amounts were based on each farmer's previous three years of harvests. In the Dust Bowl, many small farmers and those who grew only minimal amounts of wheat, mostly for their own use, believed it was not worth participating in the program. "After all the administrative formulas were completed, the average national wheat acreage reduction was 15 percent," Paul Bonnifield says. In some southern states, the cotton crop was reduced by about 25 to 50 percent.

When the AAA did not work, successive acts were put in place, including the Soil Conservation and Domestic Allotment Act of 1936, and the Agricultural Adjustment Act of 1938. Over time, the three federal government programs did help to improve the economy of the Dust Bowl, and many farmers who might have lost everything managed to survive as a result of U.S. government assistance. Yet as a whole, the federal government's relief efforts in the Dust Bowl were a failure. One reason is because none of the three acts were designed to assist the smallest farmers—those who most needed help. About 50 percent of Dust Bowl farmers produced about 17 percent of the region's wheat. Of the $97 million the AAA gave to southern Plains farmers in 1933, small farmers who agreed to reduce production received only $1.5 million. The great majority of AAA funds went to those who produced a greater proportion of the wheat in the Dust Bowl—the large farmers, who could better weather the tough times in the first place.

An unintended consequence of the AAA program, therefore, was to squeeze out small farmers, especially tenant farmers and sharecroppers, who didn't own the land they farmed and were thus hardest hit by the Depression and droughts. Even though the government stipulated that AAA relief recipients were forbidden to evict tenants, many owners did so anyway. The landowners guessed correctly that government officials could not—or would not—do anything about it. "I let 'em all go," said one Oklahoma farmer. "In '34 I had I reckon four renters and I didn't make anything. I bought tractors on the money the government give me and got shet o' my renters. You'll find it everywhere all over the country thataway. I did everything the government said—except keep my renters. The renters have been having it this way ever since the government come in."

In 1937 Congress attempted to remedy this inequity by passing the Bankhead-Jones Farm Tenancy Act. The act created the Farm Security Administration (FSA), which strived to remove tenant farmers from relief rolls and give them land and loans to start anew. The well-meaning measure was unfortunately not comprehensive enough. Says one historian: "The FSA was surprisingly effective even though it was under-funded. . . . [B]ecause of its minimal budget it could assist only one applicant in twenty-two." Another reason federal aid for Dust Bowl farmers was not as helpful as it could have been was that it almost immediately began purchasing land from those who most needed the relief. The farmers most needed federal aid to keep their farms, in other words, were having their land purchased by the government.

The AAA program had other flaws as well. It made no provisions to help slow wind erosion, a huge problem in 1933. Not until the massive dust storm of May 1934, which dumped Plains topsoil on Washington, DC, itself, did U.S. officials begin to realize the seriousness of the problem. Suitcase farmers also had a great deal to do with increasing wind erosion: absent from their land, they did nothing to stop it, and some even gave up planting altogether. The erosion spread to neighboring lands—and as more lands were abandoned by suitcase farmers, the wind erosion problem worsened. By purchasing land itself, the federal government in effect became yet another absentee landlord; as a result, despite its relief efforts, the AAA was actually exacerbating the problem.

The government's claims that the Plains heartland was a one-crop area, almost totally dependent on soil-depleting wheat, was also wrong. Although wheat production boomed during World War I, Dust Bowl harvests also included significant sorghum, broom corn, and other crops.

Cattle were also very important to the region's economy. The Jones-Connally Relief Bill of April 1934 allowed the United States to purchase cattle that farmers could no longer afford to keep. But because a

The AAA program was fraught with flaws, including the fact that it made no provisions for the devastating problem of erosion in the Dust Bowl. The federal government purchased land but left it abandoned, which increased levels of erosion.

sudden oversupply of beef would drive down American market prices, the government destroyed most of the animals. Many farmers who could no longer feed their livestock had no alternative but to hand over their cattle for destruction, a sometimes heart-wrenching decision. Melt White remembers the government paying his family $16 per cow and $3 per calf, and the sorrow one felt when turning over the animals: "Well, that cow, you'd milked her," he explains. "See her big ol' kind eyes and she furnished you milk and food and—and to see 'em just take and lead her off and you knew that'as the end of her, that'as the end of her life, well, when was yours comin', you know? It was pretty sad."

Sometimes, though, the cattle were so ill that the only choice was to put them down anyway. Phyllis Hills Brantl's family cows were relatively healthy, but she vividly recalls the day the neighbors' cattle were shot. The endless rifle cracks were unnerving. It was, she says, "the worst day I ever lived."

Emotionally difficult though it could be, the drought cattle-purchasing program helped many farmers get back on their feet financially. The government bought more than eight million cattle nationwide, and beef prices increased soon afterward. In addition, the program indirectly helped to reduce soil erosion in some areas, because it reduced the stress on overgrazed land. It was by far the most successful of the Dust Bowl federal government programs.

Suffering farmers also needed a way to pay off their loans, mortgages, and taxes. The Federal Land Bank (established in 1916) and the Land Bank Commissioner Loans (established in 1933) were the two major sources of credit for farmers, but their loan policies excluded high-risk farmers who most needed help. Those who managed to secure loans were often forced by bad harvests and depressed economic conditions to default on mortgage payments. They hoped to renew the loans, but most assumed they were not prohibited from doing so. In the meantime, however, the Federal Resettlement Administration offered to buy land from those who defaulted. Some farmers, despairing of ever being able to pay their mortgages and fearful of losing their farms altogether, sold them to the Resettlement Administration—only to learn afterward that the Land Bank did renew most of their loans. Many historians sharply criticize the goals of the Resettlement Administration, noting that because the economy was no worse off in the Dust Bowl than in other parts of the country during the Depression, there was no justification for removing destitute farmers from their land. Although the federal government offered other kinds of relief, such as "feed and seed" loans, administrative red tape and numerous snafus made these loans mostly ineffective when they were most needed.

Work relief programs established during the Great Depression fought high unemployment by providing funds that paid workers to build parks, schools, bridges, and other public structures. Work relief in the Dust Bowl began with the Civil Works Administration (CWA), but President Roosevelt shut down the unproductive program after only a few months, and replaced it with the Federal Emergency Relief Administration (FERA). FERA had been formed in 1933 with a budget of $3 million earmarked for state aid. The transition from CWA to FERA was terribly disorganized, however, and FERA took months to establish programs in the Dust Bowl.

One of the reasons for the delay in the Plains was that the government favored more heavily populous areas when deciding where to begin work projects. Small towns or areas with few residents received no relief money at all. Many began moving to the larger towns and urban areas as a result, hoping for better job opportunities. The small towns suffered even more from the outflow of people; businesses closed or were forced to lay off employees. An unintended result of the federal works programs was that the most economically depressed towns often suffered even more from the effects of the programs.

In mid-1935, FERA shut down its operations in the Dust Bowl—ironically, just when national media attention was drawn to the region. FERA was replaced by the Resettlement Administration, whose main goal was to resettle farmers from the Dust Bowl area on land that was supposedly more fertile. In reality, however, the Resettlement Administration paid low prices for valuable land, and it moved families to undeveloped farms where they were forced to start from scratch on land that was worth less than the land they left.

The Works Progress Administration (WPA), created in 1935 to succeed a less expansive program begun by President Herbert Hoover, was one of the most famous relief programs of the Roosevelt's "New Deal" era. The WPA provided jobs for more than eight million people and built thousands of parks, schools, libraries, and other public buildings. Today the WPA is best known for employing artists in music, literature, theater, and other arts. Through the Arts Section, the WPA touched the lives of more than 150 million Americans. In the heart of the Dust Bowl, however, WPA operations were limited and not enough to lift a five-state area out of an economic depression. For example, it took two years after a local WPA project was approved before the work actually began and people started earning wages. The WPA's activities in the Dust Bowl lasted only 18 months.

Work-relief and farm-relief programs for Dust Bowl residents had mixed results: on the one hand, they undoubtedly helped many families who otherwise may not have survived on their own. On the other hand, the often hastily established programs had so many difficulties that they often could not accomplish even a fraction of what they set out to do. Still, all of them were the result of President Franklin D. Roosevelt's strong belief that the federal government has a duty to help Americans weather bad times. No one knew what would work, he reasoned, so it would never hurt to experiment, to keep trying to fix the problem.

And another enormous problem in the Dust Bowl was erosion. How could farmers or the government— or anyone, for that matter—combat the loss of millions of tons of rich topsoil to wind? The federal government aimed to tackle the problem by returning much of the Great Plains to grass. But this was no help to farmers— they would end up being removed from their land. Moreover, no one was quite sure how to re-seed the prairie in the first place. Experts estimated that it would take between 20 and 50 years to return cultivated land to its original state. In the meantime, the land lay empty, prey to wind erosion.

Dust Bowl farmers did not wait for the U.S. government to take action. In March 1934, residents of the Texas panhandle formed the Four-County Wind Erosion Control Association. In Kansas, too, farmers pressured local governments to require landowners to maintain their land rather than abandon it. By this time Dust Bowl farmers had learned that practices such as overtilling, "dry mulching," and burning off stubble were clearly causing erosion. No one knew for sure, however, how to prevent the topsoil from eroding down to the hardpan, the calcium carbonate layer that forms in extremely dry climates and prevents roots from taking hold. Nor did they agree on what to do after the hardpan was already exposed. In addition, they needed to address the problem of farms that had already been abandoned.

After the great roller of May 1934 dropped tons of dirt on the East Coast, the federal government decided to step in. It set up an "experiment station" in Texas to study the causes and prevention of wind erosion in the area. First, U.S. officials advised farmers—and paid them—to plow lister rows. The list plow, in wide use before the one-way disc plow became popular, throws up a ridge of dirt to each side of a furrow, creating a trough about 18 inches wide and seven inches deep. Crops are planted in the bottom of the trough. To prevent wind erosion, however, the rows must be plowed at right angles to the prevailing winds—but this often meant that they were plowed downslope and were thus more prone to water erosion. Conversely, "contour rows," which followed the natural shape of the land, often ran *with* the wind, worsening the problem.

One solution was devised by Charles Peacock, a Dust Bowl farmer who invented and patented a damming machine in 1931. The machine put "checks" in lister rows—small dams that prevented wind from carrying away soil. Peacock's machine and others like it were in use in the Dust Bowl by 1936. Another machine that helped prevent soil erosion was the pitter, which punched small, deep holes in the soil at equal intervals. Both of these machines prevented wind erosion by conserving soil moisture, which helped to raise a cover crop.

But crops still needed time to grow—and the wind was still blowing. Fred Hoeme, an Oklahoma panhandle farmer, was using a cultivator that dropped clods of earth on the surface of the ground. The hard lumps acted as windbreaks and kept water from flowing freely—but they didn't penetrate below the dusty surface. So in 1935, Hoeme developed the Hoeme Chisel, a device that treated a strip of land 16 feet wide. The chisel had two sizes of heads, one that brought up clods from deep in the soil, and another that made more shallow furrows, similar to a list plow. Farmers could use the chisel, however, in February or March when the wind started; it could also be used in April or May when the rains set in. The machine was very effective in combating both wind and water erosion.

In contrast to these home-grown efforts, the federal Soil Conservation Service was unable to develop new methods of wind erosion prevention despite its efforts. The SCS wanted to plant sorghums after listing, but this had no real effect on wind erosion. It suggested terracing, in which hillsides are cultivated with several steps, or terraces, cut into the slope, but this was far less effective in semi-arid regions than in more humid areas to the east: the tops of the terrace rows themselves became a source of wind erosion and actually worsened the problem. Strip cropping—alternating rows of grain crops with those of legumes—was another farming method popular in more temperate areas, but it did not help prevent erosion in the Dust Bowl.

One of the most effective efforts of the New Deal was the formation of the Civilian Conservation Corps (CCC). The CCC employed three million young single men to help conserve America's natural resources. Across the country, they dug irrigation ditches, planted trees, blazed

(continued on page 96)

HUGH HAMMOND BENNETT: THE FATHER OF SOIL CONSERVATION

In March 1934, a bill to create a new federal agency called the Soil Conservation Service (SCS) was introduced in Congress. A congressional committee called on Hugh Bennett, a soils expert, to testify on the need for such an agency. Bennett was to appear before Congress on May 12, 1934.

Two thousand miles away, a dust storm was raging in the Great Plains. Weather forecasters predicted that the effects of the storm would reach Washington on May 12—and Bennett knew it. He dragged out his testimony as long as possible until the storm "rolled in like a vast steel-town pall. . . . The skies took on a copper color. The sun went into hiding. The air became heavy with grit." Bennett now had concrete proof of the disaster occurring on the Great Plains. "This," he told congressmen, "is exactly what I've been talking about." Discussing the "timeliness" of the dust storm, Bennett later explained, "I suspect[ed] that when people along the seaboard of the eastern United States began to taste fresh soil from the Plains 2,000 miles away, many of them realized for the first time that somewhere something had gone wrong with the land."

Hugh Bennett was born in 1881 on his father's 1200-acre cotton plantation in Anson County, North Carolina. He learned firsthand how an experienced farmer could efficiently manage a farm: the young Bennett helped his father dig terraces to prevent soil from washing away. Hugh earned a degree in chemistry from the University of North Carolina in 1903 and began working on field soil surveys with the U.S. Bureau of Soils. In 1905, during a trip to Louisa County, Virginia, he and a colleague made a startling observation. They saw two fields, virtually side by side, of the same soil type but in drastically different conditions. One field, lightly wooded and with a great deal of under-brush, had never been cultivated; its soil was rich and moist. The other field had been plowed and tilled for planting; the soil here was dry and hard, tightly packed and crumbly to the touch.

Bennett and his colleague coined the term "sheet erosion" to describe what they saw. Bennett began to see the same conditions nearly everywhere he traveled. Poor management of the land was causing widespread soil erosion, but no one else seemed to notice. In 1909, the Bureau of Soils issued a report that stated, "The soil is the one indestructible, immutable asset that the nation possesses. It is the one resource that cannot be exhausted; that cannot be used up." Bennett would later quip, "I didn't know so much costly misinformation could be put into a single brief sentence."

Bennett spent years documenting soil erosion problems and writing countless survey reports, papers, articles, and books on soil classification. His hard work finally paid off in 1929, when he secured $160,000 in federal funds to study erosion. By 1931, he had established 10 experimental "erosion stations" around the country. Bennett's final report proved the dire extent of the problem, and in 1933, President Roosevelt created the Soil Erosion Service (SES) and appointed Hugh Bennett as its first director. The SES established about 40 demonstration projects around the country, designed to show farmers ways to minimize soil erosion. Although many farmers were wary of the newfangled techniques the man from Washington was showing them, they took heed and the projects were ultimately successful.

Still, Bennett knew the government needed to expand its efforts to have any effect on the Dust Bowl. Politicians were not listening, however—until Bennett's testimony during the giant roller of May 12, 1934. The Soil Conservation Act establishing the SCS passed unanimously. The first of its kind in the world, it was signed into law by President Roosevelt on April 27, 1935.

As Director of the SCS, Bennett formed Soil Conservation Districts, geographic regions in which local farmers and other residents signed agreements with the government to help manage soil erosion. By the end of 1935, 22 states had Soil Conservation Districts. The idea was so popular that 3,000 of the districts are still in effect today. Fittingly, the first one was established in Anson County, NC—Bennett's birthplace.

A farm devastated by the soil erosion problems that plagued the Dust Bowl.

(continued from page 93)

trails through national parks, battled forest fires, and built reservoirs—all for $30 a month. CCC members in the Dust Bowl built shelterbelts—rows of thousands of trees meant to hold the soil and retain water. Unfortunately for Plains residents, the well-meaning program failed. Most of the CCC's trees in the drought-stricken area died, unless they were near homesteads where they could be watered and tended. Those that survived did little to prevent wind erosion.

In 1936, the AAA and the SCS launched four programs, of which three were scientifically sound and helped Dust Bowl farmers considerably. The Emergency Erosion Program paid farmers 15 cents an acre to list or chisel their land. The second program required

farmers to adopt certain soil conservation practices before they could receive any federal monies. The third encouraged "stubble mulching," which discouraged farmers from burning stubble and required them to plow it under instead.

One federal program that worked in battling the stubborn Dust Bowl conditions was the SCS's plan for re-grassing cultivated areas—but the SCS itself wasn't entirely responsible for the achievement. The grasses themselves were suffering from the widespread droughts of the 1930s, and in fact, experts did not learn how to re-grass farmland successfully until the 1940s. By then the rains had returned to the region. Nature began to re-grass abandoned farmland before humans figured out how to do it.

The same farm re-grassed. Although the federal programs enacted during FDR's New Deal era did their best to fight erosion, the rains that returned to the Dust Bowl region in the 1940s were responsible for re-grassing cultivated areas and ending erosion of the soil.

The Rains Return

In the fall of 1938 the skies over the Dust Bowl opened and rain began to fall. Farmers rejoiced because the rain meant life, and they expected their best crops in more than five years.

"When the rain came, it meant life itself," remembers Floyd Coen, a Dust Bowl survivor. "It meant a future. It meant that there would be something better ahead. . . . [Y]ou'd go out in that rain and just feel that rain hit your face. It was a—a very emotional time when you'd get rain because it meant so much to you. You didn't have false hope anymore, you knew then that you was going to have some crops."

The skies finally opened over the Dust Bowl in the fall of 1938. By this time, most farmers had learned effective methods for keeping the soil in place and retaining rainfall. Conservation techniques—some devised by the government and others by farmers themselves—were in wide practice. For the first time in 1939, the area known as the Dust Bowl began to shrink. By 1941, the land at last rebounded.

Even without several inches of topsoil, the ground remained rich in minerals, and newly adopted soil and water conservation methods allowed grain crops in the Great Plains to ripen as they hadn't done in years. Throughout the 1940s the area received better than average rainfall. As World War II broke out in Europe, the "breadbasket of the world" recovered, as did the national economy: the 1942 wheat harvest, planted on far fewer acres, surpassed even that of 1931. Bumper crops in 1943 and 1944 encouraged farmers to begin plowing land that the federal government had recently reclaimed and re-seeded as grassland. By 1945, wheatlands in the southern Plains had once again expanded by 2.5 million acres. Two years later, Plains farmers produced 958 million bushels of wheat—more than the yield of the bumper season of 1919.

Seeing a second chance at profit, suitcase farmers returned to the Great Plains in droves, buying parcels of land in 5,000- and 10,000-acre increments. Some formed corporations to purchase even bigger tracts of land. In Colorado, one "suitcase company" turned a $1 million profit on 28,000 acres of land.

In the enthusiasm over their good fortune, newly prosperous farmers began to chafe under government restrictions that had been applied during the Dust Bowl years and were still in force. "The voice of two-dollar wheat is far more persuasive than scientific facts on wind, rain, sun and soil," John Bird noted in the August 30, 1947 issue of the *Saturday Evening Post*. Despite dire warnings from agronomists (specialists in crop production and soil management), most Plains farmers believed that they now were equipped with the information and the tools to prevent another disaster like the Dust Bowl. "It is time [we] began talking back to the dust bowl prophets," declared one wealthy Kansas farmer.

Then, in 1952, the droughts returned. By 1954, dust storms on a scale that had not been seen since the 1930s struck the Plains once more. In March of that year, a black blizzard turned the skies to ink from Amarillo, Texas, to the border of Canada. President Dwight D. Eisenhower considered allotting relief funds for the Great Plains. Chastened farmers began using their list and chisel plows again in a desperate effort to prevent a repeat of the 1930s. Although the 1950s droughts lasted less than five years (ending in early 1957), it was in some ways worse than that of the Dust Bowl years. From 1954 to 1957, for example, twice as many acres were damaged by wind erosion as in the years from 1934 to 1937.

Certainly dry spells will continue to plague the Great Plains. Scientists say that the region's climate pattern is now fairly regular and predictable: although droughts may vary in length and severity, they will probably strike the Plains every 20 years or so. The experts have been right thus far, as droughts during the 1970s and 1990s have proved. According to this cycle, we might expect the next dry spell to occur in the Midwest during the second decade of the 21st century.

But could the Dust Bowl happen again? Will the rolling dust storms, the vast crop devastation, and the misery of the 1930s recur? Most experts believe that it's possible. One of the main reasons is that we continue to push the Great Plains beyond the limits that the land can withstand. As long as farmers routinely practice soil conservation techniques and do not abandon them during boom times, we can fend off another disaster on the scale of the 1930s Dust Bowl. Agricultural scientists warn, however, that it is important to pay careful attention to the way new plowing, tilling, and harvesting techniques affect the soil.

Today, most Plains farmers are not overly concerned

Most experts believe that the Dust Bowl phenomenon could happen again. Droughts are cyclical and farmers on the Plains continue to push the land to its limits.

about cyclical droughts. They point to new resources, such as deep-well pumps, special irrigation sprinklers, inexpensive aluminum piping, and other water technologies that they are certain will stave off another Dust Bowl. Others are not so sure. They point out that some of the reasons farmers are so productive today are the very reasons why another severe drought might cripple the Great Plains again. For example, most farmers specialize in basic crops such as wheat, corn, milo (a type of sorghum), and alfalfa. Should another extended dry spell hit the area, it would take about a decade to switch to more drought-resistant crops. Moreover, American farmers rely more heavily on international trade than they did in the 1930s; an economic depression in another country might affect profits in the United States.

Two of the biggest threats to Plains farmland are the result of improved farming techniques: the introduction of agricultural chemicals, and the construction of deep-water wells for irrigation. One of the most pressing concerns, not only in the Great Plains but throughout the United States, is groundwater contamination. Fertilizers, pesticides, and other agricultural chemicals either dissolve in rainwater runoff or soak into the ground. Scientists are discovering that many of these substances, which are supposed to break down into harmless elements as they sink into the soil, are reaching groundwater tables intact. Much of America's groundwater is already tainted. In the Great Plains, groundwater contamination has become especially serious. Federal and state government efforts to educate farmers or ban certain chemicals outright have been somewhat effective in the region, but the overall problem is far from solved.

Even more distressing, especially in the semi-arid Great Plains, is the danger of groundwater depletion. The Plains rest above an enormous, water-bearing layer of permeable rock, sand, and gravel called an aquifer. The Ogallala (or High Plains) aquifer stretches 174,000 miles, from the Texas panhandle to South Dakota, and varies in thickness from one to 1,300 feet. It is the largest in North America and one of the largest in the world; much of the water it holds has been there for thousands of years.

An aquifer acts much like an immense sponge: the Ogallala, which holds enough water to fill Lake Huron, not only provides drinking water to most Midwesterners but it is now also tapped to irrigate crops and water live-stock. Between 1940 and 1980, the Ogallala aquifer level fell by 10 feet on average. In some parts of Texas it dropped

The Ogallala (or High Plains) aquifer underlies an area of about 174,000 miles, and is the principle source of water for the largest agricultural area in the United States.

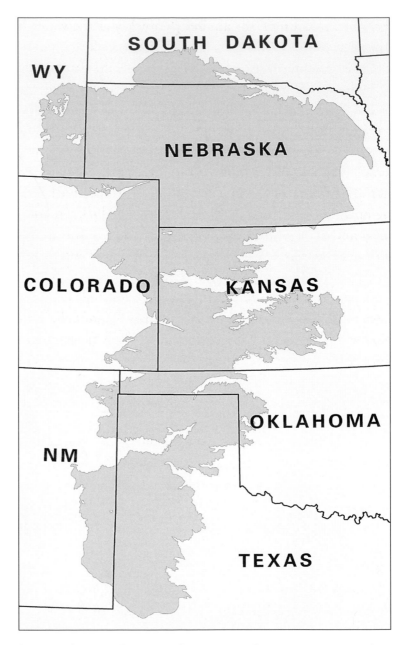

by nearly 100 feet. With improved water conservation practices and streamlined irrigation techniques, the steep decline was slowed in the 1980s. But aquifers replenish themselves with surface streams, lakes, and rainfall that seeps through the soil—and these natural processes have been unable to refill the aquifer as quickly as the water is being drawn out.

The disaster that befell the Great Plains during the 1930s—and the near-disaster of the 1950s—convinced most people that lack of knowledge or skill was not what created Dust Bowl conditions. Rather, the human factor that affected a vast region already afflicted with droughts, record heat, and staggering economic depression was the refusal to put new knowledge to good use. Farmers, scientists, and government officials learned by harrowing trial and error that a vital element of survival was maintaining effective conservation practices while increasing crop production.

Have these lessons been passed down? "You can't convince me we've learned our lesson," one Kansas farmer told his neighbors in the late 1930s. "It's just not in our blood to play a safe game."

Chronology

c. 18000–10000 B.C.	Paleo-Indians begin migrating to North America from Northeast Asia
c. 6000 B.C.	Glaciers retreat from North America for the last time; larger animals become extinct
c. 5000–1000 B.C.	Archaic period: Paleo-Indians settle in river valleys and begin diverging into tribes
1540 A.D.	Francisco Vásquez Coronado launches an expedition from present-day New Mexico to the Oklahoma panhandle and northwest to Kansas
1700	Comanches emigrate from Wyoming to the Great Plains, followed by the Kiowa, Cheyenne, and Arapaho tribes; guns and horses increase bison hunting and reduce the bison population
1803–1806	Louisiana Purchase doubles the size of the United States; Zebulon Pike is sent to explore the new territory
1862	After Congress passes the Homestead Act, thousands of settlers from the East move to the Plains
1866–1886	Oliver Loving and Charles Goodnight establish one of the first Great Plains cattle trails; settlers and cattle barons begin slaughtering bison in record numbers to make room for cattle to graze; only a few thousand bison remain on the Great Plains by the late 1880s, when the cattle industry collapses
1889	A six-year drought hits the Plains; the population of the southern Plains drops by as much as 90 percent in some areas
1900	The Reeves steam-driven plow is introduced
1909–1912	Enlarged Homestead Act encourages migration to the Great Plains (each settler now receives 320 acres); land entries soar when Congress reduces the "proving time" for homesteaders from five to three years

Chronology

1914–1918	During World War I, wheat supplies from Russia are cut off, creating a huge market for Great Plains farmers. The Food Control Act of 1917 guarantees farmers $2.00 per bushel of wheat; millions of acres of grassland are plowed and cultivated with new gas-powered tractors and plows
1919	Wheat farmers of the Great Plains have the highest yields of wheat and the greatest profits ever
1920	American wheat prices drop drastically and remain low; farmers set more grassland to wheat in an effort to break even
1929	On October 29, the stock market crashes, ushering in the Great Depression
1930	A drought begins in the East and spreads westward; between 1931 and 1937, 20 states set records for dryness that still stand
1933	Weather observers in the Texas and Oklahoma panhandles report between 70 and 140 dust storms; in November, a dust storm originating in the northern Plains states drops tons of dirt on the East Coast. Agricultural Adjustment Act establishes the Agricultural Adjustment Administration (AAA), aimed at creating a "scarcity" of grain and cotton crops to drive prices back up
1934	Heat waves that begin sweeping the Plains combine with droughts to create catastrophic conditions; the Jones-Connally Relief Bill allows the United States to purchase cattle that farmers cannot afford to keep (most are sacrificed); on May 9–12, an enormous dust storm carries more than 300 million tons of topsoil from the Plains to the Atlantic Ocean
1935	On "Black Sunday," April 14, a dust storm of unprecedented proportions blackens the skies over eastern cities; Soil Conservation Act is signed into law on April 27; 2.5 million people begin leaving the Plains states—a great number of them head for California

Chronology

1936	American farms lose as much as $25 million in profits daily and the heat kills 4,500 people
1937	Congress passes the Bankhead-Jones Farm Tenancy Act, which establishes the Farm Security Administration (FSA); its goal is to remove tenant farmers from relief rolls and give them land and loans
1938–1939	The drought ends on the Great Plains; the area known as the Dust Bowl shrinks for the first time in 1939
1942–1947	Bumper wheat crops in 1942, 1943, and 1944 persuade farmers to re-plow land claimed by the federal government for re-grassing; wheatlands have expanded by 2.5 million acres in 1945; 1947 wheat yield is highest ever
1952–1957	A drought once again strikes the Great Plains, renewing interest in soil and water conservation practices

Further Reading

Andryszewski, Tricia. *The Dust Bowl: Disaster on the Plains.* Brookfield, Conn.: Millbrook Press, 1993.

Farrell, Jacqueline. *The Great Depression.* San Diego, Calif.: Lucent Books, 1996.

Farris, John. *The Dust Bowl.* San Diego: Lucent Books, 1989.

Low, Ann Marie. *Dust Bowl Diary.* Lincoln, Neb.: University of Nebraska Press, 1984.

Nardo, Don. *Opposing Viewpoints Digests: The Great Depression.* San Diego: Greenhaven Press, 1998.

Nishi, Dennis. *The Way People Live: Life During the Great Depression.* San Diego: Lucent Books, 1998.

Press, Petra. *A Cultural History of the United States Through the Decades: The 1930s.* San Diego: Lucent Books, 1999.

Sherrow, Victoria. *Hardship and Hope: America and the Great Depression.* New York: Henry Holt, 1997.

Stanley, Jerry. *Children of the Dust Bowl: The True Story of the School at Weedpatch Camp.* New York: Crown Publishers, 1992.

Stein, R. Conrad. *The Great Depression.* Chicago: Children's Press, 1993.

Steinbeck, John. *The Grapes of Wrath.* New York: Viking Press, 1939.

Time-Life Books. *Our American Century: Hard Times: the 1930s.* Alexandria, Va.: Time-Life Books, 1998.

Further Reading

WEBSITES:

"American Buffalo: Spirit of a Nation" (PBS Online)
www.pbs.org/wnet/nature/buffalo/index.html

"Day of the Black Blizzard" (Discovery Channel Online)
www.discovery.com/area/history/dustbowl/dustbowl1.1.html#blues

The Dust Bowl in Art and History
www.mingspring.com/~jwar/dust/dustbowl.htm

"Dust Bowl Sisters" (D.J. Tice)
www.pioneerplanet.com/archive/cent/dox/cent12.htm

The Geologic Story of the Great Plains
www.lib.ndsu.nodak.edu/govdocs/text/greatplains/text.html

"The National Grasslands Story" (National Grasslands Council,
USDA Forest Service)
www.fs.fed.us/r2/nebraska/gpng/story.html

"Surviving the Dust Bowl" (PBS Online, transcript of TV program)
www.pbs.org/wgbh/amex/dustbowl/index.html

Index

Index

Picture Credits

THERESE DeANGELIS received an M.A. in English literature from Villanova University and was a contributing editor for Chelsea House's WOMEN WRITERS OF ENGLISH and MODERN CRITICAL INTERPRETATIONS series. She is the author of several books for young adults, including *Native Americans and the Spanish, Jodie Foster, New Mexico,* and *The Bombing of Pearl Harbor*; she is also co-author of *Marijuana* in Chelsea House's JUNIOR DRUG AWARENESS series. She lives near Philadelphia, PA, with six funny little birds.

GINA DeANGELIS has written more than 15 nonfiction books for children and young adults, including the award-winning Chelsea House books *The Triangle Shirtwaist Company Fire of 1911* and *The Hindenburg*. For some reason she is particularly fond of writing about disasters. Gina holds a master's degree in history, and lives in Williamsburg, VA, in a house in which the humans outnumber the gerbils three to two.

The authors would like to thank David Bianco for his formidable Internet research skills.

JILL McCAFFREY has served for four years as national chairman of the Armed Forces Emergency Services of the American Red Cross. Ms. McCaffrey also serves on the board of directors for Knollwood—the Army Distaff Hall. The former Jill Ann Faulkner, a Massachusetts native, is the wife of Barry R. McCaffrey, who served in President Bill Clinton's cabinet as director of the White House Office of National Drug Control Policy. The McCaffreys are the parents of three grown children: Sean, a major in the U.S. Army; Tara, an intensive care nurse and captain in the National Guard; and Amy, a seventh grade teacher. The McCaffreys also have two grandchildren, Michael and Jack.